VEGAN COOKING FOR EVERYONE

Vegan Cooking for Everyone

LEAH LENEMAN

Thorsons

Thorsons
An Imprint of HarperCollins*Publishers*
77–85 Fulham Palace Road,
Hammersmith, London W6 8JB

The Thorsons website address is:
www.thorsons.com

and *Thorsons*
are trademarks of
HarperCollins Publishers Limited.

The recipes in this volume have been previously
published in
The Tofu Cookbook
Easy Vegan Cooking
Vegan Cooking for One

This collection published 2001

10 9 8 7 6 5 4 3 2 1

A catalogue record of this book
is available from the British Library

ISBN 0 00 712347 7

Printed and bound in Great Britain
by The Bath Press, Bath

Contents

The Author

Leah Leneman's approach to meat- and dairy-free cooking has always been both practical and creative, providing new ways for people to enjoy delicious vegan food. Her classic titles, such as *Easy Vegan Cooking* and *Vegan Cooking For One*, have de-mystified vegan cookery and made meat- and dairy-free a straightforward option for us all. Always full of enthusiasm and energy for her interests, Leah's involvement with vegan organizations both in the U.S. and U.K. has helped raise the profile of healthy eating and vegan cooking throughout the world.

Introduction

There are many reasons people choose to eat vegan food, and these days we're wise enough to know that healthy eating doesn't need to mean a drastic change of lifestyle. Some of you may choose to "go vegan", entirely removing meat and dairy products from the kitchen and your life, whilst others prefer to "dip in" with the occasional vegan meal. Whatever your choice you'll feel the health benefits and enjoy the food!

Vegan Cooking For Everyone is exactly what it says it is. It's a hallmark of Leah Leneman's work that there's a generous range of dishes that will appeal to all sorts of diners – young and old, the adventurous and fussy-eaters alike. Best of all Leah has ensured there is a host of "look alike" dishes and extra special desserts so no one need feel deprived of their meat and dairy staples.

In the past questions have been asked of the vegan diet. *"Is it safe?"* *"Will I get enough protein?"* *"Will I get the full range of nutrients without meat and dairy?"* Today, research has demonstrated that a balanced vegan diet is better than safe – it's positively good for you. Nutritionists, and medical doctors alike now sing the praises of a diet low in saturated fats, low in cholesterol, low in added sugar and high in fresh vegetables and plant proteins. So it's official – the vegan diet is one of the healthiest you could choose.

Medical research has confirmed that "we are what we eat" – and health professionals now recognize the role of diet in preventing modern-day diseases such as Alzheimer's, cancer, heart disease, diabetes, asthma, and allergic reactions. It's also suggested that the simple vegan diet can help with the symptoms of P.M.S., menopause, and premature aging.

This book is a collection of the very best of Leah Leneman's recipes, gathered together from her previously published works. One of the first internationally successful vegan cookery writers, Leah Leneman was a true pioneer of healthy eating. Her accessible meat- and dairy-free recipes are now classics and we know she would be both delighted and proud to see this new color illustrated collection available – *For Everyone!*

Soups, Snacks, and Salads

Soups

Soups make a superbly healthy, quick to prepare light meal. They're versatile too – ranging from thick full broths to keep you warm through winter, to light, cool summer soups. Either way it's always satisfying to prepare and serve your own soup.

No Fat Lentil and Smoked Tofu Soup

SMOKED TOFU ADDS A NEW DIMENSION TO AN OLD-FASHIONED LENTIL SOUP.

³/₄ cup/6 oz/170g smoked tofu

2 cloves garlic

3³/₄ cups/30 fl oz/850ml water

³/₄ cup/4 oz/115g red lentils

2 cloves

2 tablespoons chopped parsley

³/₄ pound/340g potatoes

Freshly ground black pepper as
required

Sea salt as required (optional)

1 Dice the tofu finely. Mince the garlic.

2 Put the water, lentils, tofu, garlic, cloves, and parsley in a
saucepan and bring to a boil.

3 Scrape or peel the potatoes and dice them very finely. Add
them to the saucepan. Lower the heat, cover the saucepan
and simmer for about 20 minutes, by which time both
lentils and potatoes should be very soft. Add pepper to taste
(salt should not be necessary, but add a little sea salt if it is).
If you prefer a smoother consistency, put the cooled soup in
the blender and then reheat. Serve immediately.

Lentil and Barley Soup

THE COMBINATION OF LENTIL AND POT BARLEY (THE UNREFINED VERSION OF PEARL BARLEY) MAKES THIS A HIGH-PROTEIN, SUSTAINING SOUP, PERFECT FOR A WINTER DAY. IT IS ALSO GOOD FOR SLIMMERS AS IT IS FAT FREE.

$^2/_3$ cup/4 oz/115g brown lentils

$^1/_3$ cup/2 oz/50g pot barley

1 large onion

2 sticks celery

2 carrots

5 cups/40 fl oz/1120ml water

2 teaspoons dried mixed herbs

1 tablespoon miso

1 Cover the lentils and barley with boiling water and leave to soak for a few hours or overnight. Drain well and rinse thoroughly.

2 Chop all the vegetables finely.

3 Mix together the lentils, barley, and chopped vegetables and cover them with water. Bring to a boil, adding the herbs.

4 Simmer for 30–40 minutes until the lentils and barley are tender. Remove a little of the liquid and mix thoroughly with miso until smooth. Return this to the saucepan, mix thoroughly and serve. (Miso is quite salty, but extra salt can be added if desired.)

Lentil and Dulse Soup

DULSE IS A HOME-GROWN SEA VEGETABLE WHICH GIVES A LOVELY FLAVOR TO SOUP.

2 onions
2 cloves garlic
2 tablespoons vegetable oil
1 cup/6 oz/170g red lentils
5 cups/20 fl oz/1120ml water
1 vegetable bouillon cube
1 oz/30g dulse
Sea salt as required
Freshly ground black pepper as
   required

1 Chop the onions and garlic finely. Sauté in the oil in a
   saucepan 3–4 minutes.

2 Rinse and add the lentils and water; bring to a boil. Crumble
   and stir in the bouillon cube.

3 Chop the dulse and add it to the saucepan. Turn heat as low
   as possible, cover pan and simmer for 20–30 minutes,
   stirring occasionally. Taste for seasoning, add sea salt if
   necessary (some stock cubes are quite salty) and freshly
   ground black pepper to taste.

Tofu Vichyssoise

TOFU TRANSFORMS A CLASSIC FRENCH RECIPE, WHICH WOULD MAKE A GOOD APPETIZER FOR
A DINNER PARTY.

4 leeks

1 onion

$^1/_4$ cup/2 oz/55g vegan margarine

1 pound/455g potatoes

1 tablespoon paprika

4 cups/35 fl oz/1 liter vegetable
 bouillon or water

3 tablespoons soy sauce

Freshly ground black pepper as
 required

1 cup/$^1/_2$ pound/225g soft or medium
 tofu

Chopped chives or scallions as
 required

1 Chop the leeks and onion finely. Sauté in the margarine for
 15–20 minutes over a low heat until tender.

2 Peel the potatoes, or leave the skins on if preferred, and dice
 them. Add them to the saucepan with the bouillon or water,
 soy sauce, and black pepper. Bring to a boil, then cover and
 simmer for about 20 minutes, until the potatoes are soft.
 Cool slightly.

3 Put the mixture into a liquidizer with the tofu and blend
 thoroughly.

4 Chill, and serve sprinkled with chopped chives or scallions.

Avocado Vichyssoise

THIS IS AN UNUSUAL VARIANT ON AN OLD FAVORITE. SUITABLE FOR A DINNER PARTY.

3 leeks

1 large onion

2 tablespoons vegan margarine

1 pound/455g potatoes

3³/₄ cups/30 fl oz/850ml water

¹/₂ vegetable bouillon cube

1 avocado

²/₃ cup/5 fl oz/140ml soy milk

¹/₄ teaspoon freshly grated nutmeg

Sea salt as required

Sprinkling of paprika

1 Chop the leeks and onion. Sauté for 3–4 minutes in the margarine.

2 Peel and slice the potatoes thinly. Add to the leek and onion.

3 Pour in the water and add the bouillon cube. Bring to a boil, then cover and simmer for about 15 minutes until tender. Set aside to cool.

4 Peel and chop the avocado. Place in liquidizer and add the leek, potato mixture, and milk. Also add the nutmeg and salt. Blend thoroughly.

5 Place in the refrigerator until thoroughly chilled. Sprinkle with paprika before serving.

Chilled Carrot Soup

THIS IS A PLEASANT SOUP FOR A HOT SUMMER DAY.

1 pound/455g carrots

1¹/₃ cups/10 fl oz/285ml water

2 tablespoons grated onion

4 tablespoons peanut butter

2¹/₂ cups/20 fl oz/570ml soy milk

Sea salt as required

Freshly ground black pepper as required

1 Clean and slice the carrots, cover them with the water and boil gently for 20 minutes.

2 Add the grated onion and peanut butter and simmer for 20 minutes more.

3 Cool slightly, add milk and seasoning, then blend the soup in a liquidizer.

4 Chill for several hours before serving.

Tomato Bisque

A BISQUE IS A CREAMY SOUP THAT RETAINS THE TEXTURE OF THE MAIN INGREDIENT.

2 onions

2 cans (14–16 oz/400g each) tomatoes

1¹/₂ cups/12 fl oz/340ml water

1 cup/¹/₂ pound/225g soft or medium tofu

1 tablespoon vegan margarine

Sea salt and freshly ground pepper as required

1 Chop the onions finely. Put them into a saucepan with the tomatoes (chop them coarsely with a spoon while adding them – or use canned chopped tomatoes), the water, and seasonings. Bring to a boil, then lower the heat and simmer, uncovered, for 20–30 minutes.

2 Put the tofu into a liquidizer with the margarine and a few spoonfuls of liquid from the soup. Blend thoroughly.

3 Add the contents of the liquidizer to the saucepan. Heat gently over a very low heat and serve immediately.

Vegetable Soup

THIS SOUP IS IDEAL FOR THOSE WHO PREFER A SOUP IN WHICH THE INGREDIENTS REMAIN RECOGNIZABLE.

2 onions

3 carrots

2 sticks celery

1 tablespoon vegan margarine

5 oz/140g canned tomato paste

1 vegetable bouillon cube

5 cups/40 fl oz/1120ml water

Sea salt as required

Freshly ground black pepper as required

1 oz/30g whole-wheat spaghetti

$\frac{1}{8}$ cup/2 oz/55g fresh or frozen green beans

1 cup/4 oz/115g cabbage

2 heaped tablespoons whole-wheat flour

1 Slice the onions, carrots, and celery.

2 Melt the margarine and add the vegetables, sautéeing gently for 3–4 minutes without browning. Stir in the tomato paste, bouillon cube, water, salt, and pepper.

3 Bring to a boil and simmer for 10 minutes.

4 Break the spaghetti into small pieces, add to the soup and simmer for 10 minutes.

5 Shred the cabbage and beans. Add them to the soup and simmer for 5–10 minutes until the spaghetti is tender.

6 Mix the flour with a little cold water in a cup. Add this to the soup, stirring well, and cook for another minute before serving.

Potato and Carrot Potage

FOR THOSE WHO LIKE A BLENDED SOUP, THIS ONE SHOULD PROVE A FAVORITE, AS THE POTATOES GIVE IT A PLEASANT CREAMINESS.

$1\frac{1}{2}$ pounds/680g potatoes
1 pound/455g carrots
1 small onion
$\frac{1}{3}$ cup/3 oz/85g vegan margarine
5 cups/40 fl oz/1120ml water
Sea salt as required
Freshly ground black pepper as required
Grated nutmeg as required
Chopped parsley as required

1 Peel the potatoes and cut them into slices. Slice the onion and carrots.
2 Melt half the margarine, add the onion and cook until softened but not brown. Add the potatoes and carrots and stir well.
3 Add a little salt and the water and cook until the vegetables are tender.
4 Cool slightly, then put into a liquidizer and purée.
5 Return the soup to the pan, reheat and season to taste. Stir in the remaining margarine and a little freshly chopped parsley.

Cream of Mushroom Miso Soup

TRADITIONAL MISO SOUPS ARE NOT CREAMY, BUT THERE IS NO REASON WHY THIS INGREDIENT SHOULD NOT BE USED IN A NON-TRADITIONAL SOUP. IT SHOULD NOT BOIL AFTER THE MISO IS ADDED. SUITABLE FOR A DINNER PARTY.

8 cups/1 pound/455g mushrooms
1 onion
2 sticks celery
$^1/_4$ cup/2 oz/55g vegan margarine
2 cups/15 fl oz/425ml water or
  vegetable bouillon
2 tablespoons miso
2 tablespoons whole-wheat flour
2 cups/15 fl oz/425ml soy milk
Freshly ground black pepper as
  required
3 tablespoons finely chopped parsley

1 Chop the mushrooms, onion, and celery. Melt half the margarine in a saucepan and add the vegetables. Sauté for about 3 minutes.

2 Add the water or bouillon, bring to a boil, then lower the heat, cover and simmer for about 10 minutes.

3 Pour the mixture into a liquidizer along with the miso and leave to cool slightly. Blend thoroughly.

4 Meanwhile, melt the remainder of the margarine and stir in the flour. Gradually stir in the milk, very slowly to avoid lumps, and bring to a boil. Boil for a minute or two, then lower heat to the barest minimum and pour in the contents of the liquidizer.

5 Season with pepper, and serve topped with the parsley.

Cream of Celery Soup

THIS CREAMY SOUP IS NOT ONLY LOW IN FAT BUT LOW IN CALORIES AS WELL. SERVE IT TO WEIGHTWATCHERS — AND ANYONE ELSE WHO ENJOYS A GOOD SOUP.

1 head celery

1 onion

2 tablespoons vegetable oil

4 cups/35 fl oz/1 liter water or vegetable bouillon

Sea salt as required

Freshly ground black pepper as required

1 teaspoon dried mixed herbs

1 cup/1/2 pound/225g soft or medium tofu

2 tablespoons chopped parsley

1 Wash and chop the celery. Chop the onion. Sauté both in the oil for a few minutes.

2 Add the water or bouillon, seasoning, and herbs. Bring to a boil, then lower the heat, cover and simmer for about 20 minutes.

3 Pour into a liquidizer and leave to cool slightly. Add the tofu and blend thoroughly.

4 Pour back into the saucepan and reheat gently. Serve topped with parsley.

Cream of Cauliflower and Potato Soup

COMBINING TOFU WITH POTATO AND CAULIFLOWER GIVES A RICH CREAMINESS THAT IS MORE USUALLY ASSOCIATED WITH AN UNDESIRABLY HIGH FAT CONTENT.

1 small cauliflower

1 onion

1 pound/455g potatoes

3³/₄ cups/30 fl oz/850ml vegetable bouillon or water

1 cup/¹/₂ pound/225g soft or medium tofu

Sea salt as required

Freshly ground black pepper as required

1 tablespoon vegan margarine

Chopped parsley as required

1 Chop the cauliflower, onion, and potatoes into dice, cover and cook in the bouillon or water until very soft. Cool briefly, then pour into a liquidizer, add the tofu and blend thoroughly.

2 Return the mixture to the saucepan, add seasoning and the margarine and reheat gently. Serve topped with chopped parsley.

Wakame and Miso Soup

WAKAME IS A SEA VEGETABLE TRADITIONALLY USED IN JAPANESE MISO SOUPS.

1 oz/30g dried wakame

1 large onion

2 tablespoons vegetable oil

4 cups/35 fl oz/1 liter water

2–3 teaspoons miso

1 Soak the wakame in cold water for about 10 minutes. Drain and chop.

2 Chop the onion finely and sauté in the oil until lightly browned. Pour in the water and bring to a boil. Add the wakame, lower the heat, then cover the pan and simmer for 10–15 minutes.

3 Remove a little of the liquid from the pan and mix it in a small bowl with the miso. Return it to the pan, leave the pan uncovered on the lowest possible heat for a minute or two then serve immediately.

Chestnut and Celery Soup

THE COMBINATION OF CHESTNUT AND CELERY HAS LONG BEEN POPULAR, AND WORKS WELL AS A SOUP.

2 onions

4 sticks celery

2 tablespoons/1 oz/30g vegan margarine

2 cups/15 fl oz/425ml vegetable bouillon or water

1/2 pound/225g dried chestnuts which have been soaked in a thermos flask (see page 104)

1 1/3 cups/10 fl oz/285ml soy milk

Sea salt as required

Freshly ground black pepper as required

1 Chop the onions and celery finely. Heat the margarine in a saucepan and sauté them for a few minutes.

2 Add the bouillon or water and bring to a boil. Chop the chestnuts coarsely and add them to the pan. Lower the heat, cover and simmer for 10–15 minutes.

3 Pour the milk into a liquidizer and add about half the soup mixture. Blend thoroughly and return to the pan, stirring well. Season to taste. Simmer over a low heat for a few minutes longer before serving.

Coconutty Corn and Bell Pepper Soup

THIS DELICIOUS SOUP HAS A SWEET FLAVOR REMINISCENT OF MALAYSIAN CUISINE. A QUICK RECIPE.

2 onions

3 tablespoons vegetable oil

1 red bell pepper

2 cloves garlic

1–2 teaspoons ground ginger

3¾ cups/30 fl oz/850ml water

½ pound/225g fresh, frozen, or
   canned corn

½ cup/4 oz/115g creamed coconut,
   chopped or grated

Sea salt as required

Freshly ground black pepper
   as required

1 Chop the onions finely. Sauté in the oil for a few minutes.

2 Chop the bell pepper finely and add it to the saucepan.
   Mince the garlic and stir it in. Sauté for a few minutes
   longer.

3 Add the ginger to the pan and stir well. Pour in the water
   and bring to a boil. Add the corn and creamed coconut. Add
   seasoning to taste. Cover the pan and simmer for a few
   more minutes before serving.

Gumbo

DEEP-FRYING TOFU MAKES IT LIGHT AND CHEWY, ADDING A TERRIFIC TEXTURE TO SOME CLASSIC SOUPS.

1 cup/$^1/_2$ pound/225g medium or
  firm tofu
2 tablespoons vegetable oil plus
  additional for deep-frying
1 onion
1 small green bell pepper
$^1/_2$ pound/225g ladies' fingers
1 can (14–16 oz/400g) tomatoes
3$^3/_4$ cups/30 fl oz/850ml vegetable
  bouillon or water
1 bay leaf
2–3 tablespoons chopped parsley
Sea salt as required
Freshly ground black pepper
  as required

1 Chop the tofu into small dice and deep-fry in the oil until
   golden brown. Drain well and set aside.
2 Chop the onion and bell pepper. Clean the ladies' fingers, top
   and tail them and chop each one into 2–3 pieces. Sauté these
   ingredients in the 2 tablespoons oil for 4–5 minutes, stirring
   occasionally.
3 Add the tomatoes, bouillon or water, and bay leaf to the
   ladies' fingers mixture, bring to a boil, then lower the heat,
   cover and simmer for 15–20 minutes.
4 Add the fried tofu, parsley, and seasoning, cook for a couple
   of minutes longer, then serve.

Snacks, Dips, and Spreads

Healthy snacks are an important part of our daily diet. Often it's when there isn't time to stop and have a full meal that we fill ourselves up on high-fat, high-sugar, low-nutrition comfort snacks. These bite-sized treats and fresh dips are perfect top ups for throughout the day – and also make wonderful tasters for parties or dinner guests.

Spicy Potato Balls

THIS MAKES A PLEASANT APPETIZER OR LUNCH DISH. IT IS A GOOD WAY OF USING UP LEFTOVER COOKED POTATOES AND SERVES FOUR FOR LUNCH OR EIGHT TO TEN AS AN APPETIZER. SERVE WITH CHUTNEY.

1¹/₂ pound/680g potatoes

2 onions

1 tablespoon vegan margarine

2 fresh green chilies

1 in/2.5cm piece fresh ginger

2 teaspoons mustard seeds

2 tablespoons broken cashews

Sea salt as required

Juice of ¹/₂ lemon

1¹/₂ cups/6 oz/170g chick pea flour

1 cup/8 fl oz/225ml water

1 Cook the potatoes; cool, peel, and mash.

2 Chop the onions finely. Heat the margarine in a large saucepan, add the onions and sauté them for a few minutes. Peel and chop the chilies (making sure to discard all the seeds) and ginger finely. Add them to the pan and cook for a couple of minutes longer. Add the mustard seeds and cashews and continue cooking for a few minutes more.

3 Remove the pan from the heat and add the mashed potatoes, a little salt, and the lemon juice. Mix well, then form into little balls about the size of walnuts.

4 Mix the chick pea flour and water and add a pinch of salt. Coat the potato balls in the batter and deep-fry them until they are golden.

Millet and Cashew Patties

THESE TASTY PATTIES CAN BE SERVED WITH PLAIN SOY YOGURT OR A TOMATO SAUCE.

2 large onions
2 tablespoons vegetable oil plus
    additional for frying
2 cups/8 oz/225g millet, cooked
1 cup/4 oz/115g cashews
8 tablespoons nutritional yeast flakes
    or powder
Sea salt as required
Freshly ground black pepper as
    required

1 Chop the onion finely. Heat 2 tablespoons of the oil in a
    saucepan and sauté the onion for about 3 minutes.
2 Add the cooked millet to the pan and mash it well. Stir
    briefly, then remove from the heat.
3 Grind the cashews. Add them to the millet, along with the
    yeast and seasoning. Mix well and form into 16 patties.
4 Fry the patties in a little oil in a skillet until lightly browned
    on both sides.

Hijiki Tofu Balls

THIS IS A SUBSTANTIAL SEA VEGETABLE-BASED SNACK. THE BALLS ARE PARTICULARLY NICE SERVED
WITH A DIP MADE FROM SOY SAUCE AND FINELY GRATED FRESH GINGER, DILUTED WITH WATER TO TASTE.

2 oz/55g hijiki
2½ cups/1¼ pounds/565g tofu
4 tablespoons soy sauce
1–2 (about 4 oz/115g) carrots
Sesame seeds as required
Oil for deep-frying as required

1 Rinse the hijiki well by covering with water and draining two or three times. Soak it in enough water to cover for about 20 minutes.

2 Bring the water to a boil, lower the heat and simmer the hijiki for about 20 minutes. Add 2 tablespoons soy sauce and simmer for 15–20 minutes. Drain and cool.

3 Drain the tofu, put it into a large bowl and mash thoroughly. Grate the carrot. Chop the hijiki finely. Add the carrot and hijiki to the tofu, along with the remaining soy sauce. Knead the mixture with the hands, then form into balls about the size of golf balls.

4 Spread sesame seeds on to a plate and roll each ball in them so that they are coated with the seeds.

5 Deep fry the balls until lightly browned.

Falafel Bites

THE SECRET OF THIS RECIPE IS TO USE RAW BEANS, NOT COOKED ONES. SERVE THEM IN PITTA BREAD POCKETS, WITH SHREDDED LETTUCE AND FINELY CHOPPED CUCUMBER AND TOMATO, WITH SOME TAHINI CREAMED WITH LEMON JUICE AND MINCED GARLIC.

$1^{1}/_{3}$ cups/$^{1}/_{2}$ pound/225g garbanzo beans

6 scallions

2 teaspoons coriander seeds

2 teaspoons cumin seeds

1 clove garlic

2 teaspoons chopped parsley

1 teaspoon sea salt

1 teaspoon baking soda

Freshly ground black pepper as required

Vegetable oil for frying as required

1 Cover the garbanzo beans with cold water and leave to soak overnight. Drain well and grind the beans – in a food processor, liquidizer (do them in at least 4 separate batches), or mincer.

2 Chop the scallions finely. Grind the coriander and cumin. Mince the garlic.

3 Combine all the remaining ingredients with the garbanzo beans in a large bowl. Mix thoroughly.

4 Form the mixture into small balls about the size of a walnut. Deep-fry them in oil which has been heated to 350–375°F/180–190°C (or in a deep-fat fryer) until they are golden. Drain thoroughly on paper towels.

Tomato and Onion Savory

FOR A QUICK LUNCH OR SNACK, NOTHING COULD BE SIMPLER OR TASTIER THAN THIS. A QUICK RECIPE.

2 large onions

12 medium-sized or large very ripe
   tomatoes

1/4 cup/2 oz/55g vegan margarine

Pinch of dried oregano

2 teaspoons raw cane sugar

Sea salt as required

Freshly ground black pepper
   as required

8 slices whole-wheat toast spread
   with vegan margarine

1　Slice the onions and chop the tomatoes coarsely.

2　Heat the margarine and sauté the sliced onions until golden. Add the tomatoes and seasonings.

3　Simmer gently for approximately 15 minutes until the tomatoes are tender.

4　Serve immediately on hot "buttered" toast.

Grilled Garlic Mushrooms

THIS IS AN IDEAL LIGHT LUNCH OR SNACK FOR LOVERS OF MUSHROOMS AND GARLIC. A QUICK RECIPE.

8 cups/1 pound/455g mushrooms

1/2 cup/4 oz/115g vegan margarine

2 cloves garlic

8 small slices whole-wheat toast

1　Clean the mushrooms and remove the stems.

2　Mince the garlic and sauté it in the margarine over a very low heat.

3　Fill the mushrooms with the garlic–margarine mixture. Place in a shallow baking dish and broil for 5–7 minutes.

4　Soak up the margarine which has run out of the mushrooms with the toast; place the mushrooms on the toast and serve hot.

Wakame Fritters

THIS SEA VEGETABLE MAKES A TASTY SNACK.

1 cup/4 oz/115g whole-wheat flour
2 teaspoons baking powder
1 teaspoon cream of tartar
²/₃ cup/5 fl oz/140ml water
1 teaspoon soy sauce
1 teaspoon vegetable oil
2 oz/55g wakame
Oil for deep-frying as required
Slices of lemon as required

1 Mix the flour with the baking powder and cream of tartar. Whisk in the water, soy sauce, and vegetable oil. Let the batter stand for at least half an hour.
2 Soak the wakame for about 10 minutes. Drain and chop into pieces, discarding any tough central rib. Coat the pieces with the batter and deep-fry until crisp.
3 Drain the fritters well, keeping them warm, and serve with lemon slices.

Kombu Fritters

KOMBU HAS A VERY DIFFERENT TASTE AND TEXTURE FROM WAKAME BUT ALSO MAKES LOVELY FRITTERS.

Fritter batter (see recipe for Wakame Fritters above)
2 oz/55g kombu
Oil for deep-frying as required
Slices of lemon as required

1 Make the batter as described in the recipe for Wakame Fritters. Leave for at least half an hour.
2 Soak the kombu for about 10 minutes. (If a less chewy texture is desired then cook it for 20–30 minutes, drain, and cool before using.) Chop the kombu into small pieces, coat with batter and deep-fry until crisp.
3 Drain well, keeping the fritters warm, and serve with lemon slices.

No-dairy Rarebit

THIS IS AN AMERICAN VERSION OF AN OLD BRITISH FAVORITE. THOSE WHO DO NOT HAVE ACCESS TO A VEGAN HARD CHEESE CAN USE A SPREAD INSTEAD. A QUICK RECIPE.

2 jars (235g each) vegan cheese spread or 1 cup/$\frac{1}{2}$ pound/225g hard vegan cheese, grated
$\frac{2}{3}$ cup/5 fl oz/140ml soy milk
1 teaspoon vegan Worcestershire sauce
Pinch of mustard powder
Pinch of cayenne pepper

1 Gently heat all the ingredients in a saucepan. Serve on toast as soon as it is blended, smooth, and bubbling.

Fried Peanut Butter Sandwiches

YOU MAY HAVE ALREADY THOUGHT OF THIS SIMPLE RECIPE, BUT FOR THOSE OF YOU WHO HAVEN'T IT'S AN EASY AND QUICK LUNCH DISH. SERVE WITH CRISP LETTUCE LEAVES.

8 slices whole-wheat bread
Peanut butter as required
Vegan margarine or vegetable oil

1 Spread half the slices of bread thickly with peanut butter. Cover with the dry slices.
2 Heat the margarine or oil in a skillet and fry the sandwiches, turning them once so they are lightly browned on both sides. Serve immediately.

Tofu Piperade

SERVE ON TOAST OR ON BROWN RICE OR WITH POTATOES OR — FOR AN EASY SAVORY FLAN — IN A PRE-BAKED PIE SHELL.

1 large onion
2 cloves garlic
1 green bell pepper
1 red bell pepper
4 tablespoons extra virgin olive oil
4 large tomatoes
$^1/_2$ teaspoon dried thyme
$^1/_2$ teaspoon dried oregano
Sea salt as required
Freshly ground black pepper as required
$1^1/_2$ cups/$^3/_4$ pound/340g tofu
$^1/_2$ teaspoon turmeric

1 Slice the onion thinly, mince the garlic cloves, and thinly slice the bell peppers.
2 Sauté the above in the oil until tender but not brown.
3 Peel and chop the tomatoes. Add them to the pan along with the herbs and seasoning.
4 Cook, stirring occasionally, for about 10 minutes.
5 Mash the tofu with the turmeric and add to the pan. Cook for several minutes more, stirring constantly, until the mixture is well heated.

Spicy Tofu Scramble with Bell Pepper and Tomato

THIS IS ANOTHER "SCRAMBLED" TOFU DISH: IN THIS ONE THE TOFU IS MADE DRIER BY SQUEEZING OUT EXCESS MOISTURE. SERVE ON TOAST.

1 onion

1–2 cloves garlic

2 tablespoons vegan margarine

2 red bell peppers

1 pound/455g tomatoes

2–3 cups/1¼–1½ pound/565–680g tofu

2–3 tablespoons soy sauce

1–2 teaspoons Tabasco sauce

1 Slice the onion thinly. Chop the garlic finely. Sauté in the margarine for about 3 minutes.

2 Chop the bell peppers finely. Add to the skillet, lower the heat from medium to low, cover the pan and leave to simmer for 3–5 minutes.

3 Peel and chop the tomatoes. Put the tofu into a clean dish towel and squeeze the moisture out. Add the tomatoes and tofu to the skillet, with the soy sauce and Tabasco sauce; raise the heat and stir until everything is piping hot.

Eggplant Toasties

2 medium eggplants

2 large onions

3 tablespoons olive oil

Sea salt as required

Freshly ground black pepper as required

Whole-wheat toast

1 Cut the eggplants in half from top to bottom and lay them cut side down on a baking dish. Bake at 400°F/200°C/Gas Mark 6 for about half an hour, by which time they should be soft. Leave to cool.

2 Slice the onion thinly. Fry the sliced onion in the olive oil in a skillet until lightly browned.

3 Scrape the eggplant flesh from the skin and discard the skin. Chop the flesh coarsely. Add it to the skillet and continue cooking for a couple of minutes longer. Season to taste and serve immediately over hot toast.

Tofu Guacamole

THERE ARE MANY VERSIONS OF THIS MEXICAN CLASSIC, BUT THE IDEA OF ADDING TOFU INSTEAD OF HIGH-FAT, CALORIE-LADEN SOUR CREAM IS COMPARATIVELY NEW.

1 ripe avocado

1 clove garlic

1 cup/½ pound/225g medium or soft tofu

Juice of ½ lemon

2 tablespoons vegetable oil

2 teaspoons soy sauce

4 tablespoons water

1 Peel and dice the avocado. Mince the garlic.

2 Either mash all the ingredients together or place in a liquidizer and blend. Serve immediately.

Hummus

IT MAY BE EASY TO FIND READY-MADE HUMMUS THESE DAYS, BUT NOTHING BEATS THE HOME-MADE ONE. THE ADDITION OF CUMIN SEEDS MAKES THIS VERSION SUPERIOR. A QUICK RECIPE.

2½ cups/1 pound/455g or 2 cans (14–16 oz/400g each) cooked garbanzo beans

2 cloves garlic

Juice of 1 large lemon

2 tablespoons tahini

2 tablespoons cumin seeds

3–5 tablespoons bean liquid

Sea salt as required

1 Drain the beans, reserving the liquid.

2 Put all the ingredients into a liquidizer and blend well. It will usually be necessary to scrape the sides a few times to get an even blend. For a thick solid hummus add only about 3 tablespoons of the cooking liquid from the beans; for a thin runny dip add more.

No-dairy Egg Mayo Spread

IN THIS RECIPE TOFU IS USED RAW AS A SANDWICH FILLING IN PLACE OF EGGS. A QUICK RECIPE.

1 cup/$^1/_2$ pound/225g tofu

$^1/_4$ teaspoon turmeric

1 stick celery

1 small onion

1 tablespoon vegan mayonnaise

1 tablespoon finely chopped parsley

1 teaspoon nutritional yeast

$^1/_2$ teaspoon mustard powder

Sea salt (or celery salt) as required

1 Mash the tofu. Finely chop the onion and celery.

2 Combine all the ingredients and store in the refrigerator.

Lentil Pâté

IT IS DIFFICULT TO KNOW WHEN SOMETHING IS A PÂTÉ RATHER THAN A SPREAD BUT THE TEXTURE AND RICHNESS OF THIS AND THE RECIPE WHICH FOLLOWS SEEM TO DEMAND THE PÂTÉ LABEL.

4 oz/115g whole-wheat bread
1/2 cup/4 oz/115g red lentils
1 1/3 cups/10 fl oz/285ml water
1 onion
2 tablespoons vegetable oil
1 tablespoon tahini
1 teaspoon dried rosemary
1/2 teaspoon dried thyme
Pinch of nutmeg
1 tablespoon finely chopped parsley
1 tablespoon miso

1 Break the bread up into pieces, cover with water and leave to soak for about an hour.
2 Cook the lentils in the water for about 15 minutes until tender.
3 Chop the onion. Sauté it in the oil for about 5 minutes until tender and beginning to brown.
4 Add the onions to the lentils. Drain the bread and squeeze as much moisture out as possible; add to the lentils and onions.
5 Stir in the tahini, rosemary, thyme, and nutmeg and cook over a low heat for about 5 minutes.
6 Stir in the parsley and miso, beating well to amalgamate it into the mixture.
7 Turn into an oiled baking dish, and bake for about half an hour at 350°F/180°C/Gas Mark 5. Serve warm or cold.

Pecan Pâté

THIS PÂTÉ CAN BE SERVED ON TOAST OR CRISPBREAD OR, ALTERNATIVELY, THE MIXTURE CAN BE FORMED INTO LITTLE BALLS AND SERVED WITH SALAD. (VECON IS A CONCENTRATED VEGETABLE STOCK PASTE.)

1 cup/4 oz/115g pecans

2 cups/4 oz/115g whole-wheat
  bread crumbs

1 large carrot

1 small onion

1 tablespoon chopped parsley

2 teaspoons tomato paste

1 teaspoon Vecon

1 tablespoon hot water

1 Grind the pecans.

2 Grate the carrots finely. Chop the onion finely. Dissolve the Vecon in the hot water.

3 Combine all the ingredients in a bowl and, using your fingers, mix them well. Cover the bowl and refrigerate for two hours or longer.

Navy Bean and Olive Dip

ALTHOUGH HUMMUS IS PROBABLY THE MOST WELL-KNOWN BEAN-BASED DIP, IN THE MIDDLE EAST YOU WILL FIND MANY OTHERS SUCH AS THIS RECIPE. A QUICK RECIPE.

2½ cups/1 pound/455g or 2 cans
   (14–16 oz/400g each) cooked
   drained navy beans
Juice of 2 small lemons
8 black olives
4 tablespoons olive oil
Sea salt as required
Freshly ground black pepper
   as required

1 Drain the beans and blend them thoroughly in a liquidizer, with the lemon juice.
2 Chop the olives finely and add them to the puréed beans, along with the olive oil and seasoning to taste. Stir well so that the mixture is thoroughly amalgamated.
3 Cover and refrigerate until serving time.

Eggplant and Tahini Dip

THIS IS ANOTHER MIDDLE-EASTERN CLASSIC, WHICH APPEARS UNDER VARIOUS NAMES (BABA GANOUSH IS ONE) AND WITH VARIANTS OF INGREDIENTS IN DIFFERENT COUNTRIES. CHARRING THE EGGPLANTS IS ESSENTIAL FOR THE FLAVOR OF THIS DISH. SUITABLE FOR A DINNER PARTY.

4 small or 2 large (about 2 pound/900g) eggplants

3 cloves garlic

2 tablespoons tahini

Juice of 2 lemons

Sea salt as required

Freshly ground black pepper as required

3 tablespoons finely chopped parsley

1 Prick the eggplants all over with a fork. Place them under a hot broiler and broil them, turning when necessary, until they are thoroughly charred on all sides (a fork should pierce right through them with no resistance). An alternative method is to bake them in a very hot oven 450°F/230°C/Gas Mark 8 for about an hour. This is obviously the longer and more costly method in fuel, but the oven method works best for large eggplants and the broiler method for small ones.

2 Rinse the eggplants under cold water and peel the charred skins off. (This does not have to be done immediately; if preferred they can be left to cool first.)

3 Chop the eggplant flesh. Chop the garlic. Put both into the liquidizer along with the tahini, lemon juice, salt, and pepper. Blend thoroughly.

4 Stir the parsley in last. Serve either chilled or at room temperature.

Tempeh Spread

THIS HAS A SIMILAR THEME TO THE PREVIOUS RECIPE, BUT IS A LITTLE MORE ELABORATE.

1 cup/½ pound/225g tempeh

1 large onion

2 cloves garlic

2 tablespoons vegetable oil

4 tablespoons soy bakon bits

1 teaspoon oregano

5 tablespoons minced parsley

5–6 tablespoons vegan mayonnaise

1 Steam the tempeh, then mash it in a mixing bowl.

2 Chop the onion finely, mince the garlic, and sauté together in the oil in a skillet for 3–5 minutes until lightly browned.

3 Add the fried onion and garlic to the tempeh, together with the soy bakon bits, oregano, parsley, and mayonnaise. Mix thoroughly. Chill before serving.

Cauliflower Sandwich Spread

MIXING THE WHITE FLESH OF A FOWL OR FISH WITH MAYONNAISE IS A POPULAR METHOD OF MAKING A SANDWICH FILLING. THIS RECIPE USES THE SAME METHOD BUT WITH A WHITE VEGETABLE INSTEAD.

1 medium cauliflower
4 scallions
2 tablespoons minced parsley
4–5 tablespoons vegan mayonnaise

1 Wash and break the cauliflower into florets. Steam in a small amount of water for a few minutes until just tender.

2 Mash the cauliflower coarsely or chop it finely. Cool it. (Alternatively the cauliflower can be cooked the day before and left in the refrigerator overnight, to be mashed just before eating.)

3 Chop the scallions finely.

4 Combine all the ingredients and if they are not already chilled then chill before serving.

Crunchy Garbanzo Spread

THIS SIMPLE RECIPE IS USEFUL WHEN YOU NEED TO PREPARE SOMETHING FROM STORECUPBOARD INGREDIENTS. A QUICK RECIPE.

2¹/₂ cups/1 pound/455g or 2 cans
   (14–16 oz/400g each) cooked
   garbanzo beans
3 sticks celery
4 scallions
4 tablespoons vegan mayonnaise
Sea salt as required
Freshly ground black pepper
   as required

1 Drain the beans. Place them in a large bowl and mash them. They do not have to be particularly smooth.
2 Chop the celery and scallions finely.
3 Combine all the ingredients and use immediately or chill before serving.

Salads

Salads are as fresh as good food gets. The vitamin and mineral content of our food is highest before it's been cooked up — so the more you keep your fruit and vegetables raw the better the benefits for your health.

Kidney Bean Pasta Salad

THIS IS A HIGH-PROTEIN, FILLING MAIN DISH SALAD.

$2^1/_2$ cups/1 pound/455g cooked kidney
beans or 2 cans (14–16 oz/400g
each) kidney beans

2 cups/$^1/_2$ pound/225g whole-wheat
pasta shapes

4 sticks celery

$^1/_2$ green bell pepper

4 scallions

$^2/_3$ cup/3 oz/85g walnuts

Sea salt as required

Freshly ground black pepper as
required

5 tablespoons vegetable oil

3 tablespoons cider vinegar or wine
vinegar

2 (or more) tablespoons soy bakon bits

Crisp lettuce leaves as required

1 Drain the beans. Cook the pasta, rinse in cold water and
drain. Combine the pasta and beans.

2 Chop the celery, bell pepper, and scallions finely. Chop the
walnuts coarsely.

3 Add the vegetables and nuts to the pasta and bean mixture.

4 Combine the oil, vinegar, and seasoning. Add this to the
salad and mix well.

5 Turn the mixture into a lettuce-lined bowl, sprinkle with
soy bakon bits and serve.

Caribbean Salad

THIS SALAD IS BEST SERVED AS AN APPETIZER OR ACCOMPANIMENT RATHER THAN A MAIN DISH.
A QUICK RECIPE.

¹/₂ green bell pepper
¹/₂ red bell pepper
4 sticks celery
1 can (14–16 oz/400g) pineapple
    chunks
4 tablespoons coarsely chopped
    walnuts
4–6 tablespoons vegan mayonnaise
Lemon juice as required

1 Chop the bell peppers and celery and drain the pineapple.
2 Combine all the ingredients and serve.

Garbanzo and Walnut Salad

THIS IS A HIGH-PROTEIN MIDDLE-EASTERN MIXTURE WHICH SERVES FOUR AS A LUNCHEON DISH OR EIGHT
AS AN APPETIZER. A QUICK RECIPE.

2¹/₂ cups/1 pound/455g or 2 cans
    (14–16 oz/400g each) cooked
    drained garbanzo beans
³/₄ cup/4 oz/115g walnuts
6 tablespoons lemon juice
4 tablespoons vegetable oil
2 cloves minced garlic
1 teaspoon sea salt
Hearts of 2 heads Romaine lettuce

1 Drain the beans. Mash them until they are the consistency
of coarse crumbs.
2 Chop the walnuts finely and combine them with the
mashed beans.
3 Combine the lemon juice, oil, garlic, and salt and mix this
dressing with the walnuts and beans.
4 Serve at room temperature, spooned into the center of a
shallow dish. Surround with lettuce leaves to use as
scoopers.

Green Bean and Almond Salad

IN MEDITERRANEAN COUNTRIES COOKED VEGETABLES ARE OFTEN DRESSED WITH OIL AND VINEGAR AND SERVED COLD AS SALADS, BUT THE ADDITION OF NUTS AND RAISINS IN THIS RECIPE MAKES IT DISTINCTIVE AND GIVES IT MORE SUBSTANCE. IT SERVES FOUR AS A LIGHT LUNCHEON DISH OR EIGHT AS AN APPETIZER.

1 pound/455g fresh or frozen green
  beans
$^1/_2$ cup/2 oz/55g almonds
4 tomatoes
1 small onion
2 tablespoons/1 oz/30g vegan
  margarine
$^1/_3$ cup/2 oz/55g raisins or golden
  seedless raisins
2 tablespoons vegetable oil
2 tablespoons cider vinegar or wine
  vinegar
Sea salt as required
Freshly ground black pepper
  as required

1 Wash, string, and slice the beans and cook them until tender. Drain them well and leave to cool.
2 Shred the almonds finely. Peel and chop the tomatoes and onions.
3 Melt the margarine in a saucepan, add the onion, almonds, and raisins and sauté them until the onion is tender.
4 Combine the oil, vinegar, and seasoning.
5 Mix together the beans, onion mixture, tomatoes, and dressing in a bowl.
6 Chill and serve.

Potato and Artichoke Salad

CANNED ARTICHOKES ARE QUITE EXPENSIVE, BUT THEY MAKE THIS MEDITERRANEAN-STYLE SALAD SOMETHING SPECIAL. COLD-PRESSED EXTRA VIRGIN OLIVE OIL SHOULD, OF COURSE, BE USED.

1 pound/455g potatoes
½ cup/2 oz/55g walnuts
1 can (14–16 oz/400g) artichoke hearts
4 tablespoons extra virgin olive oil
Sea salt as required
Freshly ground black pepper as required
2 teaspoons lemon juice
Crisp lettuce leaves as required

1 Cook the potatoes until tender. (They can be peeled if desired, but this is not necessary.) Quarter them and sprinkle with 1 tablespoon extra virgin olive oil while still warm.
2 Chop the walnuts and combine them with the potatoes.
3 Drain the canned artichoke hearts and arrange them on lettuce leaves with the potatoes and walnuts.
4 Combine the remaining extra virgin olive oil with the lemon juice and seasoning and pour over the salad.

Salad Niçoise

IN RESTAURANTS THIS TRADITIONAL SALAD IS NORMALLY BARRED TO VEGETARIANS BECAUSE IT CONTAINS ANCHOVIES: HERE CAPERS ARE USED INSTEAD TO ADD A PIQUANT, SALTY TASTE.

1 pound/455g fresh or frozen French beans
2 large potatoes
6 large tomatoes
4 tablespoons extra virgin olive oil
2 tablespoons cider vinegar or wine vinegar
¼ teaspoon mustard powder
Sea salt as required
Freshly ground black pepper as required
1 tablespoon capers
½ cup/2 oz/55g olives

1 Cook the beans and potatoes (separately) until tender. Leave to cool and slice them.
2 Quarter the tomatoes and arrange them with the beans and potatoes on individual salad plates.
3 Combine the extra virgin olive oil, vinegar, mustard, and seasoning and pour this over the salad.
4 Chop the olives finely, combine them with the capers and sprinkle over the salad.

Green Bean and Pimento Salad

CANNED PIMENTOS ARE RARELY USED FOR ANYTHING MORE THAN A GARNISH, THOUGH THEY HAVE A LOVELY, SWEETISH FLAVOR. THIS IS A SIDE SALAD RATHER THAN A MAIN DISH.

1 can (8 oz/225g) pimentos
1 cup/1 pound/455g fresh or frozen
   sliced green beans
2 carrots
4 tablespoons vegan mayonnaise

1 Drain the pimentos and slice them into thin strips.
2 Cook the beans until just tender; drain and leave to cool.
3 Grate the carrots coarsely.
4 Combine all the ingredients and serve.

Tabbouleh

NO VEGAN COOKERY BOOK WOULD BE COMPLETE WITHOUT A VERSION OF THIS MIDDLE-EASTERN CLASSIC.

1⅓ cups/½ pound/225g bulgur wheat
2 cups/2 oz/55g fresh parsley
4 or 5 scallions
2 tablespoons fresh mint or 2
   teaspoons dried mint (optional)
Juice of 1 small lemon
4 tablespoons extra virgin olive oil
Sea salt as required
Freshly ground black pepper as
   required

1 Cover the wheat with plenty of cold water and leave to soak for 45 minutes to one hour.
2 Line a colander with a clean dish towel and pour the bulgur wheat into it, allowing the water to drain through. Gather up the edges of the towel and squeeze the wheat, to expel as much of the liquid as possible. Place in a large mixing bowl.
3 Mince the parsley, scallions, and the fresh mint if used. Add to the wheat. Pour in the lemon juice and oil and stir well.
4 Season to taste and serve.

Lentil Salad

THIS IS ANOTHER TRADITIONAL MIDDLE-EASTERN DISH. THERE IS NO NEED TO SOAK THE LENTILS BEFOREHAND.

2 onions
2 cloves garlic
Vegetable oil as required
1¹/₃ cups/¹/₂ pound/225g brown lentils
Juice of 1 lemon
2 teaspoons cumin seeds
Sea salt as required
Freshly ground black pepper
   as required

1 Chop the onions. Heat the oil in a large saucepan and sauté the onions until lightly browned.

2 Mince the garlic.

3 Add the lentils, garlic, lemon juice, and enough water to cover the lentils by about ³/₄–1 inch/2–2.5cm. Cover, bring to a boil, then lower the heat and simmer.

4 Crush the cumin seeds. After the lentils have been cooking for about 15 minutes add the cumin, salt, and pepper. Cover the saucepan again and leave to simmer for another 10–15 minutes, by which time the water should be absorbed and the lentils tender (if not, then raise the heat and uncover the saucepan).

5 Leave to cool, then chill in the refrigerator.

French Bean Salad

THIS IS A FRENCH-STYLE SALAD. OTHER FRESH HERBS CAN BE USED IN ADDITION TO, OR INSTEAD OF, PARSLEY.

1 cup/6 oz/170g dried black-eyed
   beans
Juice of 1 lemon
3 tablespoons olive oil
1½ cups/1½ oz/45g fresh parsley
Sea salt as required
Freshly ground black pepper
   as required

1 The night before, cover the beans with boiling water and leave to soak overnight.

2 In the morning, drain them, cover with lots of fresh water, bring to a boil, then lower the heat. Sprinkle in a little lemon juice, then cover and leave to simmer until tender, about 45 minutes. After about half an hour add a little more lemon juice – this prevents the beans becoming brown. A few minutes before the end of the cooking time add a little sea salt.

3 Drain the beans and, while still hot, pour the remainder of the lemon juice and the olive oil over them. Stir well. Leave to cool, then chill.

4 Chop the parsley finely. Just before serving stir the parsley into the beans and add salt and pepper to taste.

Three Bean Salad

THIS IS A TASTY VARIATION OF THE CLASSIC RECIPE.

½ pound/225g fresh or frozen green
   beans
1 onion
1⅓ cups/½ pound/225g cooked
   drained kidney beans
1⅓ cups/½ pound/225g cooked
   drained garbanzo beans
4 tablespoons extra virgin olive oil
4 tablespoons cider vinegar or wine
   vinegar
Sea salt as required
Freshly ground black pepper
   as required

1 Cook the green beans in a little salted water until just
   tender. Drain and cool. (If the beans are whole then slice
   them.)
2 Slice the onion very thinly.
3 Combine the kidney beans, garbanzo beans, and green beans
   in a bowl. Add the onion. Pour over the oil, vinegar, and
   seasoning and mix well.
4 Cover the bowl and refrigerate for several hours to marinate
   before serving.

Millet Salad

MILLET IS A VERY NUTRITIOUS GRAIN AND IN THIS RECIPE FORMS THE BASIS OF A TASTY SALAD.

$^{3}/_{4}$ cup/6 oz/170g millet

Sea salt as required

Freshly ground black pepper
   as required

$^{1}/_{2}$ green bell pepper

4 scallions

2 sticks celery

$^{1}/_{3}$ cup/1 oz/30g sunflower seeds

2 tablespoons extra virgin olive oil

1 tablespoon cider vinegar or wine
   vinegar

2 tablespoons minced parsley

1 Cook the millet until tender (about 20 minutes) in three times its volume of water, with a little sea salt added. Cool, then chill.

2 Finely chop the bell pepper, scallions, and celery. Toast the sunflower seeds under a broiler until lightly browned.

3 Fluff the millet with a fork. Add the oil and vinegar and mix in.

4 Stir in the chopped vegetables and parsley and the toasted sunflower seeds. Adjust the seasoning as required.

Fruit and Nut Coleslaw

NOW THAT VEGAN MAYONNAISE IS READILY AVAILABLE IN HEALTH FOOD SHOPS, LOVERS OF COLESLAW CAN EASILY RING THE CHANGES. A QUICK RECIPE.

1 small white cabbage

2 sweet apples

1 can (8 oz/225g) pineapple chunks

$^{3}/_{4}$ cup/4 oz/115g salted peanuts

$^{1}/_{2}$ cup/4 oz/115g vegan mayonnaise

1 Shred the cabbage and dice the apple.

2 Combine with all the remaining ingredients in a salad bowl and serve.

Piquant Coleslaw

1 head (2 pound/900g) white cabbage

4 sticks celery

1 green bell pepper

1 small onion

12 green olives

4–6 tablespoons vegan mayonnaise

A few drops Tabasco sauce

1 Grate the cabbage coarsely. Chop the celery and bell pepper. Chop the onion and olives finely.

2 Combine all the ingredients in a large bowl and mix thoroughly.

High Protein Vegetable Salad

2 cups/$^1/_2$ pound/225g white cabbage

1 large carrot

1 cup/2 oz/55g mushrooms

1 stick celery

$^1/_4$ cucumber

2 tablespoons chopped parsley

$^2/_3$ cup/4 oz/115g cooked red kidney beans

$^1/_2$ cup/2 oz/55g chopped cashews

$^1/_3$ cup/1 oz/30g sunflower seeds

3 tablespoons vegetable oil

Juice of 1 lemon

1 Grate the cabbage and carrot coarsely. Chop the mushrooms, celery, and cucumber finely.

2 In a bowl combine the cabbage, carrot, mushrooms, cucumber, parsley, beans, cashews, and sunflower seeds.

3 Pour the oil and lemon juice over the mixture and combine thoroughly.

4 Cover the bowl and leave in refrigerator until serving time.

Avocado and Mushroom Salad

AS A MAIN DISH FOR LUNCH THIS SERVES FOUR, BUT IT STRETCHES TO EIGHT AS AN APPETIZER.
SUITABLE FOR A DINNER PARTY.

4 cups/¹/₂ pound/225g mushrooms

1 clove garlic

Juice of 2 small lemons

¹/₃ cup/3 fl oz/90ml extra virgin
   olive oil

2 teaspoons mustard

4 medium avocados

4 boxes mustard and cress

1 Slice the mushrooms thinly.

2 Mince the garlic and mix with the lemon juice, olive oil, and
   mustard to make a dressing.

3 Combine the mushrooms and dressing and leave to
   marinate for about half an hour, turning occasionally.

4 Peel the avocados and slice into long thin pieces.

5 Arrange a bed of cress on four plates and arrange the
   avocado slices on top.

6 Spoon the mushroom mixture over the avocados.

Italian Pasta Salad with Smoked Tofu

THIS CAN BE MADE WITH PASTA SHELLS OR ANY OTHER PASTA SHAPE. THE SMOKED TOFU ADDS AN
APPEALING FLAVOR AND AN INTERESTING TEXTURE, AS WELL AS PROTEIN. A QUICK RECIPE.

½ pound/225g whole-wheat pasta
   shapes

2–3 scallions

1 large green or red bell pepper

12 olives

¾ cup/6 oz/170g smoked tofu

3 slices whole-wheat bread

2 tablespoons extra virgin olive oil

2 teaspoons cider vinegar or wine
   vinegar

Pinch of dried oregano

¼ teaspoon garlic salt

Freshly ground black pepper
   as required

1 Cook the pasta until tender, drain, place in a large salad bowl
   and cool.

2 Chop the scallions finely. Halve the olives and remove the
   stones. Chop the bell pepper. Dice the tofu. Toast the bread
   lightly and cube it. Add all of these ingredients to the pasta
   in the bowl.

3 In a small cup combine the oil, vinegar, oregano, garlic salt,
   and pepper using a fork. Pour the dressing over the salad,
   toss well and serve.

Valencia Salad

A SALAD WITH A MEDITERRANEAN FLAVOR. IF FRESH ASPARAGUS IS IN SEASON IT WOULD MAKE THE DISH EVEN NICER.

2 cups/³/₄ pound/340g brown rice

1 small can (6–7 oz/200g) pimentos

2–3 slices onion

1 tablespoon chopped parsley

Sea salt as required

³/₄ cup/7 fl oz/200ml virgin olive oil

4 tablespoons cider vinegar or wine
   vinegar

1 can (14–16 oz/400g) artichoke hearts

1 cup/¹/₂ pound/225g firm tofu

1 can (14–16 oz/400g) asparagus

1 Cook the rice in salted boiling water until tender. Chop the pimentos and add to the rice.

2 Mix the onion slices, parsley, and salt with the olive oil. Leave to stand for half an hour. Remove the onion slices and mix in the vinegar.

3 Stir half this vinaigrette into the rice and pimentos.

4 Chop the artichoke hearts coarsely. Marinate in the remaining vinaigrette.

5 Cut the tofu into cubes.

6 When ready to serve add the chopped artichoke hearts with their dressing to the rice, along with the cubes of tofu. Decorate with the asparagus.

Hijiki Salad with Tofu Dressing

HIJIKI (ALSO SPELLED HIZIKI) IS ONE OF THE NICEST JAPANESE SEA VEGETABLES, AND ITS TANG IS
WELL COMPLEMENTED BY A TOFU DRESSING.

1¹/₂–2 oz/45–55g hijiki

4–6 scallions

2 cups/1 pound/455g soft or
medium tofu

4 tablespoons vegetable oil

1 tablespoon cider vinegar or wine
vinegar

1 tablespoon tahini

3 teaspoons soy sauce

1 Cover the hijiki with cold water and leave to soak for about 20 minutes. Drain, rinse, and cover with fresh water in a saucepan. Bring to a boil, cover the pan, then lower the heat and simmer for about 10 minutes. Drain and rinse.

2 Chop the hijiki coarsely. Chop the scallions finely and put them in a bowl with the hijiki.

3 Put the tofu, oil, vinegar, tahini, and soy sauce in a liquidizer and blend.

4 Add this tofu dressing to the hijiki and mix thoroughly before serving.

Shredded Vegetable and Brown Rice Salad with Miso Dressing

THE LIST OF INGREDIENTS MAY BE LONG BUT THIS IS A SUBSTANTIAL DISH, PERFECT FOR A SUMMER'S DAY WHEN THERE ARE HEARTY APPETITES TO SATISFY BUT A HOT MEAL HAS NO APPEAL. VEGANS WHO DO NOT EAT HONEY COULD USE RAW CANE SUGAR OR OMIT THE SWEET TASTE ALTOGETHER.

½ cup/4 oz/115g medium or firm tofu

Vegetable oil for deep-frying as required

2 cups/¾ pound/340g brown rice

2 small or 1 large potato

2 large or 4 small scallions

1–2 cloves garlic

2 tablespoons chopped parsley

½ teaspoon mustard powder

Juice of ½ lemon

8 tablespoons vegetable oil

3 tablespoons cider vinegar or wine vinegar

1 tablespoon miso

2 tablespoons honey

3 tablespoons water

2 small or 1 large tomato

1 stick celery

⅓ cup/3 oz/85g white cabbage

½ cup/4 oz/115g raw beets

⅓ cup/3 oz/85g alfalfa sprouts

1 Dice the tofu, then deep-fry the cubes in the oil and set aside. Cook the brown rice and the potato, cool and set aside. (These preparations can be done in advance.)

2 Chop the scallions and garlic finely. Combine them with the parsley, mustard powder, lemon juice, and half the oil and vinegar; mix well with the rice. Leave to marinate in a cool place or the refrigerator for at least an hour.

3 Combine the remaining oil and vinegar with the miso, honey, and water and blend thoroughly in a liquidizer. Set aside.

4 Chop the potato, tomato, and celery. Grate the cabbage and beets. Combine the vegetables with the alfalfa sprouts and fried tofu in a large bowl and pour the miso dressing over. Mix thoroughly.

5 Use the marinated rice as a base and top with the vegetables and tofu in miso dressing.

Spicy Cauliflower and Tofu Salad

THIS SALAD HAS AN UNUSUAL COMBINATION OF FLAVORS AND TEXTURES.

1–1¼ cups/8–10 oz/225g–285g firm or medium tofu

Vegetable oil for deep-frying as required

1⅓ cups/½ pound/225g brown rice

1 small cauliflower

1 tablespoon vegetable oil

1 tablespoon cider vinegar or wine vinegar

4 tablespoons soy mayonnaise

2 tablespoons soy milk

1 tablespoons curry powder

Sea salt as required

Freshly ground black pepper as required

2 small green bell peppers

2 sticks celery

1 small onion

Lettuce as required

1 Cube the tofu and deep-fry in the oil. Cook the rice in salted boiling water. Cool both and set aside. (These preparations may be done in advance if desired.)

2 Wash and dry the cauliflower and divide it into florets. Mix the rice with the oil, vinegar, and cauliflower and set aside.

3 Combine the mayonnaise, milk, curry powder, salt, and pepper in a large bowl, add the cubes of deep-fried tofu and mix thoroughly.

4 Slice the bell peppers into thin strips. Chop the celery and onion finely.

5 Combine the rice mixture, the tofu mixture, and the chopped vegetables and serve on a bed of lettuce.

Rice and Corn Salad

MEDITERRANEAN FLAVORS PREDOMINATE IN THIS SALAD, WHICH HAS MASHED TOFU MIXED INTO IT.

1^1/$_3$ cups/^{1}/$_2$ pound/225g brown rice

1 green or red bell pepper

2 large or 4 small scallions

8 black olives

1 can (14–16 oz/400g) corn

2 teaspoons dried or 2 tablespoons
   fresh basil

1 cup/^{1}/$_2$ pound/225g firm or
   medium tofu

2 teaspoons soy sauce

^{1}/$_2$ teaspoon mustard powder

2 tablespoons cider vinegar or wine
   vinegar

2 tablespoons lemon juice

4 tablespoons virgin olive oil

Freshly ground black pepper
   as required

1–2 tomatoes

Lettuce as required

1   Cook the rice in salted boiling water until tender, then cool.

2   Chop the bell pepper. Chop the scallions and olives finely. Drain the corn and add it to the rice with the bell pepper, scallions, olives, and basil. Crumble the tofu into this mixture.

3   Combine the soy sauce, mustard powder, vinegar, lemon juice, oil, and black pepper and stir well with a fork.

4   Add this dressing to the rice and mix thoroughly. Leave for at least an hour in a cool place or the refrigerator.

5   Slice the tomatoes. Serve the salad piled on to lettuce leaves and top with the sliced tomatoes.

Rice, Bell Pepper, and Tofu Salad

A REALLY QUICK AND EASY DISH — ESPECIALLY IF THE RICE HAS BEEN COOKED IN ADVANCE AND REFRIGERATED.

1²/₃ cups/10 oz/285g brown rice

1¹/₄–1¹/₂ cups/10–12 oz/285g–340g firm or medium tofu

4 scallions

1 large green bell pepper

2 tablespoons chopped parsley

4 tablespoons vegetable oil

2 tablespoons lemon juice or cider vinegar

¹/₂ teaspoon garlic salt

Lettuce as required

Sliced tomatoes as required

1 Cook the rice in salted boiling water until tender then leave to cool.

2 Mash the tofu. Chop the scallions finely. Slice the bell pepper thinly. Add these ingredients to the rice together with the parsley and mix well.

3 Combine the oil, lemon juice or vinegar, and garlic salt and add to the rice mixture, stirring in thoroughly.

4 Serve on lettuce leaves, garnished with sliced tomatoes.

High Health
Main Dishes

The wholesome ingredients in these main course dishes are the staple of a good diet. Low in saturated fats but high in all the right slow-burning fuels, these fabulous vegan recipes will ensure you stay lean, healthy and full of energy throughout your day.

Rice & Grains

RICE

So many vegan dishes are wonderful served with rice so it's not surprising that it appears often in this collection. Rice is the perfect complement to protein-rich foods such as beans or tofu and a combination of the two makes for maximum nutritional benefit.

Many different varieties of rice are available from around the world. In these recipes short grain is not distinguished from long grain, although short grain rice is perhaps more suitable for Oriental cooking than long.

GRAINS

Barley – a pleasantly "nutty" grain which can be used as a base for many dishes in place of rice. The best barley is "pot barley" which is to pearl barley what brown rice is to white. To cook pot barley, cover with boiling water and soak for several hours. Then discard the soaking water, rinse the barley, and cover with fresh water, adding a little salt. Bring the fresh pot to a boil then cover the pan and simmer for about 25 minutes.

OATS These were the staple food of the Scots for centuries. Not eaten in their grain form, oats are usually seen as "meal" or as flakes.

MAIZE The word "corn" originally meant any kind of grain, but as maize was the only grain which the first white settlers found in America the word corn came to mean maize. Unlike any other grain in this chapter, maize is eaten fresh as a vegetable rather than as a dried grain. Ground down as "cornmeal" however, it comes into its own as the basis for many delicious dishes.

MILLET This is a highly nutritious grain. It needs no pre-soaking although it will gain extra flavor if dry-roasted in a heavy pan prior to cooking. To cook it should be covered with about three times its quantity of water, with a little salt added, and simmered in a covered pan for about 30 minutes.

WHEAT Although most commonly eaten as bread and dough after having been ground down into wheat flour, wheat "berries" can be eaten whole and are similar to brown rice. The wheat berries should be pre-soaked and cooked in the same way as brown rice.

BULGAR WHEAT This is wheat that has been cracked and briefly pre-cooked. It can be cooked various ways. You can soak the bulgar wheat in cold water for 30 minutes, then drain and eat it raw, or you can cover with about three times its quantity of water then simmer for just a few minutes or until the water is absorbed. Cous cous is similar to bulgar wheat, but in this case the wheat has been refined.

Whole-wheat Pastry

THIS BASIC RECIPE FOR WHOLE-WHEAT PASTRY WILL BE FOUND IN MANY OF THE RECIPES WHICH FOLLOW.

2 cups/½ pound/225g whole-wheat
    flour
Pinch of sea salt
½ cup/4 oz/115g vegan margarine
Water as required

1 Put the flour in a bowl and add a little salt. Add the margarine in small pieces. A hard margarine is best rubbed in with a pastry blender while a fork is more suitable for a soft margarine.
2 Add enough water to make a soft dough – the amount will vary according to the type of flour used. Ensure the dough is not too firm as this will result in hard chewy pastry. If it is a little too soft then sprinkle a lot of flour on the board which will then be absorbed by the pastry, but be sure to err on the side of soft and moist.
3 Handle the dough as little as possible and roll it out on a floured board. For a pre-baked shell prick the pastry all over with a fork and bake at 425°F/225°C/Gas Mark 7 for 5–10 minutes, then for about 15 minutes at 350°F/180°C/Gas Mark 4.

Creamy Banana Risotto

THIS IS AN UNUSUAL COMBINATION BUT IT TASTES DELICIOUS.

1¼ cups/½ pound/225g brown rice
¼ cup/2 oz/55g vegan margarine
1 small onion
1 green bell pepper
¼ cup/1 oz/30g whole-wheat flour
2½ cups/20 fl oz/570ml soy milk
¼ cup/1 oz/30g vegan hard cheese
1 pound/455g green-tipped bananas

1　Cook the rice until tender.

2　Chop the onion, slice the bell pepper into thin strips, and sauté them in 2 tablespoons/1 oz/30g margarine until tender.

3　Stir this mixture into the cooked rice.

4　Melt the rest of the margarine and stir in the flour. Slowly add the milk, stirring constantly to avoid lumps. Bring to a boil and simmer for 1 minute. Add the "cheese" and stir until melted.

5　Peel and slice the bananas thinly and mix in with the rice mixture. Season to taste.

6　Put a layer of the rice mixture into an oiled baking dish. Cover with a layer of sauce. Repeat the layers until all the ingredients are used up, ending with the sauce.

7　Bake in a moderate oven at 350°F/180°C/Gas Mark 4 for about half an hour. Alternatively, cover with wax paper and microwave for about 8 minutes.

Spanish Rice

TOFU MAY NOT BE AN AUTHENTIC SPANISH INGREDIENT, BUT IF A SPANIARD TASTED THIS HE OR SHE WOULD FEEL AT HOME.

2 cups/³/₄ pound/340g brown rice

1 large onion

1 large or 2 small green bell peppers

2 cloves garlic

4 tablespoons olive oil

1 can (14–16 oz/400g) tomatoes

1¹/₃ cups/10 fl oz/285 ml vegetable bouillon or water

¹/₂ teaspoon saffron

Sea salt as required

Freshly ground black pepper as required

2 cups/1 pound/455g firm tofu

2 tablespoons/1 oz/30g vegan margarine

1 can (7¹/₂ oz/200g) pimentos

²/₃ cup/4 oz/115g fresh (shelled) or frozen peas

1 Cover the rice with boiling water and leave to soak for several hours.

2 Chop the onion and bell peppers; mince the garlic. Sauté in the olive oil in a saucepan until just tender.

3 Drain the rice and add to the pan, with the tomatoes and bouillon or water. Bring to a boil, then stir in the saffron and seasoning. Lower the heat and simmer.

4 Cut the tofu into cubes. Sauté in the margarine until golden. Add to the rice mixture and stir well.

5 Chop the pimentos. When the rice is tender and the liquid nearly absorbed – 15–20 minutes – add the pimentos and peas. Cook for 3–4 minutes before serving.

Stuffed Bell Peppers

RICE-FILLED BELL PEPPERS ARE NOT UNCOMMON, BUT HERE IS A VERY DIFFERENT STUFFING. SERVE THE PEPPERS WITH BOILED OR BAKED POTATOES.

4 green bell peppers

1 onion

2 large tomatoes

3 tablespoons vegan margarine

2 cans (12 oz/340g each) creamed-style corn

1 teaspoon sea salt

1 cup/2 oz/55g whole-wheat bread crumbs

1 Cut a slice from the stem end of the bell pepper and scoop out the seeds and dividing membranes. Boil for about 2 minutes in boiling water then drain thoroughly.

2 Chop the onion, peel and chop the tomatoes, and sauté both in 2 tablespoons of the margarine until softened.

3 Add the creamed corn and salt and heat to bubbling.

4 Stuff the mixture into the pepper cases.

5 Melt the remaining tablespoons of margarine and toss the bread crumbs in this.

6 Sprinkle the bread crumbs over the peppers and place them in an oiled, shallow baking dish.

7 Bake in a fairly hot oven at 400°F/200°C/Gas Mark 6 for about half an hour, until the peppers are tender.

Rice and Vegetable Savory

IN THIS DISH THE RICE ABSORBS THE TOMATO JUICE, FORMING A PLEASANT CONTRAST TO THE LAYERED VEGETABLES.

1³/₄ cups/10 oz/285g brown rice

1¹/₃ cups/10 fl oz/285ml tomato juice

Water as required

4 large carrots

1 pound/455g fresh or frozen
   shelled peas

2 large eggplants

4–6 tablespoons vegetable oil

1 Pour boiling water over the rice and leave to soak for several hours. Drain, place in a saucepan and add the tomato juice, 1 tablespoon of oil, and enough water to cover. Bring to a boil, lower the heat and simmer until the liquid is absorbed and the rice is tender.

2 Dice the carrots and cook them with the peas in boiling salted water until just tender. Set aside to drain.

3 Dice the eggplants and fry them in the rest of the vegetable oil until tender.

4 Place half the rice in an oiled baking dish. Cover this with the vegetables and top with another layer of rice. Press down slightly.

5 Bake in a moderate oven at 350°F/180°C/Gas Mark 4 for 15–20 minutes. Alternatively, cover with wax paper and microwave for about 6 minutes.

Fragrant Spiced Rice

THIS RICE DISH IS NICE SERVED SIMPLY WITH CHAPATIS AND CHUTNEY.

1¼ cups/½ pound/225g brown rice

1 onion

2 tablespoons vegetable oil

2 cloves garlic

2 teaspoons finely chopped fresh
   ginger

¼ cup/4 oz/115g green beans

2 cups/4 oz/115g mushrooms

1 teaspoon turmeric

2 teaspoons ground coriander

1 tablespoon garam masala

2 bay leaves

2 cups/15 fl oz/425ml water

⅔ cup/4 oz/225g fresh (shelled) or
   frozen peas

Sea salt as required

1 Cover the rice with boiling water and leave to soak for
   several hours. Drain.

2 Chop the onion and sauté in the vegetable oil for 3–4
   minutes.

3 Chop the garlic finely and add it to the saucepan, along with
   the ginger. Sauté for another minute or two.

4 Top and tail the beans; break in half or into smaller pieces if
   necessary. Chop the mushrooms. Add the beans and
   mushrooms to the saucepan, along with the rice, turmeric,
   coriander, garam masala, and bay leaves. Stir briefly, then
   add water. Bring to a boil then lower the heat and leave to
   simmer.

5 After 15–20 minutes, when most of the water has been
   absorbed, add the peas. Cook for another 3 minutes, then
   serve.

Deep-fried Rice Balls with Sweet and Sour Vegetables

THIS IS A DIFFERENT WAY OF SERVING RICE, A BIT FIDDLY PERHAPS BUT WORTH IT FOR THE DELICIOUS RESULT.

FOR THE BALLS

1¾ cups/10 oz/285g short-grain
    brown rice
4–5 scallions
2 cloves garlic
3 tablespoons miso
3 tablespoons tahini
3 teaspoons finely chopped fresh
    ginger
Cornstarch as required
Vegetable oil for deep frying as
    required

FOR THE SAUCE

1 large onion
2 tablespoons vegetable oil
1 green bell pepper
1 carrot
1 can (8 oz/225g) pineapple
3–4 teaspoons raw cane sugar
1 tablespoon cider vinegar or wine
    vinegar
2 tablespoons soy sauce
6 tablespoons water
1 tablespoon cornstarch

1 To make the balls, cook the rice until tender and cool slightly.

2 Finely chop the scallions and mince the garlic then add them, along with the miso, tahini, and ginger, to the rice. Mix very thoroughly.

3 Cover the bottom of a plate with cornstarch. Form the rice mixture into balls about the size of a walnut or a little larger, and roll in the cornstarch. As the mixture is rather sloppy and sticky, it is easier to transfer a spoonful at a time of mixture to the plate, then roll it into a ball with the help of the cornstarch adhering to it. Deep-fry the balls until brown and crisp.

4 To make the sauce, chop the onion finely and sauté in the oil for about 2 minutes.

5 Chop the bell pepper and grate the carrot coarsely. Add them to the saucepan and continue cooking for 2–3 minutes.

6 Add the pineapple juice from the can, the sugar, vinegar, soy sauce, and 3 tablespoons of the water. Bring to a boil, then lower the heat, cover and simmer for a few minutes.

7 Dissolve the cornstarch in the remaining 3 tablespoons water and stir it into the vegetables until thickened.

Persian Saffron Pilaw with Carrots and Nuts

THIS DISH DOESN'T NEED ANY ACCOMPANIMENTS.

2 cups/³/₄ pound/340g brown rice

¹/₄ teaspoon saffron threads

4 cardamom pods

2 onions

¹/₃ cup/3 oz/85g vegan margarine

3 x 1 inch/2.5cm cinnamon stick
    pieces

4 cloves

Sea salt as required

¹/₂–³/₄ pound/225–340g carrots

5 dates

1 tablespoon raisins

1 tablespoon cider vinegar or wine
    vinegar

2 tablespoons lemon juice

1–1¹/₂ cups/¹/₂–³/₄ pound/225–340g
    medium or firm tofu

¹/₂ teaspoon turmeric

Freshly ground black pepper as
    required

2 tablespoons blanched slivered
    almonds

1 Cover the rice with boiling water, leave to soak for several
   hours, then drain.

2 Crush the saffron threads and soak in a little hot water for
   about 15 minutes.

3 Remove the seeds from the cardamom pods and chop 1
   onion. Melt ¹/₄ cup/2 oz/55g of the margarine in a pan and
   add the cardamom seeds, cinnamon, and cloves. Fry, stirring
   constantly, for 2 minutes. Add the chopped onion and fry,
   stirring occasionally, for several minutes, until golden
   brown.

4 Add the rice and cook over a low heat for 3–4 minutes.
   Cover with water, add the salt and the saffron water; bring
   to a boil, then lower the heat and simmer for about 15–20
   minutes until the rice is tender and the liquid absorbed.

5 Meanwhile, peel the carrots and thinly slice them
   crossways. Melt the remaining margarine in a pan, add the
   carrots and sauté for a few minutes, stirring frequently.

6 Chop the remaining onion. Add to the carrots and sauté
   until soft.

7 Chop the dates. Add to the carrot mixture with the raisins,
   vinegar, and lemon juice. Cover the saucepan, lower the heat
   and simmer for about 15–20 minutes.

8 Meanwhile, mash the tofu in a bowl with the turmeric,
   black pepper, and a little salt.

9 When the carrots are tender, add the mashed tofu and stir
   well until the tofu is thoroughly heated.

10 Serve on the pilav sprinkled with the almonds.

Jambalaya

DEEP-FRIED TOFU ADDS A "CHEWY" TEXTURE (AND PROTEIN) TO THIS RICE DISH.

2½ cups/10 oz/285g brown rice

1 cup/½ pound/225g tofu

2 onions

3 tablespoons vegetable oil

4 sticks celery

1 green bell pepper

2 cups/4 oz/115g mushrooms

2 tomatoes

2 tablespoons miso

2 teaspoons paprika

A few drops Tabasco sauce

1 cup/1 oz/30g parsley

1 Cook the rice until tender.

2 Cube the tofu and deep-fry the cubes until golden brown.

3 Chop the onions and sauté in the oil for 2–3 minutes.

4 Chop the celery, bell pepper, and mushrooms and add to the onion. Cook for another minute or two.

5 Chop the tomatoes and add to the pan; cook for 2–3 minutes before stirring in the deep-fried tofu cubes.

6 Remove the saucepan from the heat and stir in the cooked rice, miso, paprika, and Tabasco sauce. Mix well and turn into an oiled casserole dish. Bake at 300°F/150°C/Gas Mark 2 for about 45 minutes. Alternatively, cover with wax paper and microwave for about 6 minutes.

7 Chop the parsley finely and sprinkle over the dish just before serving.

Nasi Goreng

NASI GORENG SIMPLY MEANS FRIED RICE IN MALAYSIAN/INDONESIAN. THIS IS A VEGAN ADAPTATION OF THE BASIC RECIPE AND CAN BE EATEN ON ITS OWN AS A LIGHT LUNCH OR WITH ADDED STIR-FRIED VEGETABLES, PEANUTS, TOFU ETC. FOR A SUBSTANTIAL MAIN COURSE.

2 onions
2 tablespoons vegetable oil
2 tablespoons tomato ketchup
2 tablespoons soy sauce
2 teaspoons Tabasco sauce
2 cups/12 oz/340g brown rice, cooked
1 small or ½ large cucumber

1 Chop the onions. Heat the oil in a wok or skillet and fry them until turning brown.

2 Add the ketchup, soy sauce, and Tabasco sauce to the wok and stir well. Add the cooked rice and stir-fry until heated through.

3 Dice the cucumber and sprinkle it over the top.

Warming Winter Casserole

THIS IS A GOOD INTRODUCTION TO A TASTY, RARELY-USED GRAIN.

2 onions

2 carrots

1 small cabbage

1 cup/½ pound/225g millet

⅓ cup/3 fl oz/90ml vegetable oil

3¾ cups/30 fl oz/850ml boiling water

Sea salt as required

¼ cup/1 oz/30g whole-wheat flour

1⅓ cups/10 fl oz/285ml water

1–2 tablespoons soy sauce

½ cup/1 oz/30g whole-wheat bread
   crumbs

1 Chop the onions, cut the carrots into slivers, and shred the
   cabbage.

2 Sauté the millet in 2 tablespoons of the oil until it is
   beginning to brown. Cover with the boiling water, season
   and simmer for about 20 minutes.

3 Sauté the vegetables in 2 tablespoons of the oil until tender.

4 In a separate saucepan, heat the remaining oil, add the flour
   and stir well. Slowly add the water, stirring constantly to
   avoid lumps. Add the soy sauce and bring to a boil. Simmer
   for 2–3 minutes.

5 In an oiled baking dish, place alternate layers of millet,
   vegetables, and sauce, ending with a layer of sauce. Sprinkle
   with the bread crumbs.

6 Bake in a moderate oven at 350°F/180°C/Gas Mark 4 for
   about 20 minutes until the top is lightly browned.
   Alternatively, cover with wax paper and microwave for 6–7
   minutes; finish off by browning under a broiler.

Millet and Vegetable Savory

THIS MILLET DISH IS HIGH IN PROTEIN.

1 cup/$^1/_2$ pound/225g millet

3$^3/_4$ cups/30 fl oz/850ml water

Sea salt as required

4 small or 2 large leeks

4 sticks celery

2 carrots

$^1/_4$ cup/2 oz/55g vegan margarine

1$^1/_2$ cups/$^3/_4$ pound/340g tofu

2 tablespoons tahini

1$^1/_2$ tablespoons miso

Juice of 1 small lemon

2 teaspoons soy sauce

4 tablespoons soy yogurt

6 tablespoons water

1 Wash the millet, cover with the water, and lightly salt to taste. Bring to a boil, lower the heat, cover and simmer until all the water is absorbed – about 30 minutes.

2 Meanwhile, chop the leeks and celery and grate the carrots coarsely. Melt the margarine in a skillet and sauté the vegetables for about 10 minutes, stirring frequently.

3 Put the tofu, tahini, miso, lemon juice, soy sauce, yogurt, and water in a liquidizer and blend thoroughly.

4 Mix the vegetables into the millet. Pour about three-quarters of the tofu mixture in and mix thoroughly. Pour this mixture into an oiled casserole dish and pour the remainder of the tofu mixture over the top.

5 Bake at 375°F/190°C/Gas Mark 5 for 20–30 minutes, until the top is nicely browned. Alternatively, cover with wax paper and microwave for 6–7 minutes; finish off by browning under a broiler.

Bulgur Wheat and Chestnut Bake

THIS IS A VERY QUICK AND EASY DISH, WHICH ALLOWS THE SWEET FLAVOR OF CHESTNUTS TO DOMINATE.
SERVE IT WITH SEASONAL VEGETABLES.

1/2 pound/225g dried chestnuts

1 1/3 cups/1/2 pound/225g bulgur wheat

2 onions

2 tablespoons vegetable oil

1 cup/1/2 pound/225g soy yogurt

1/2 teaspoon dried marjoram

Sea salt as required

Freshly ground black pepper as
   required

1 Soak the chestnuts in a wide-rimmed Thermos flask until
   soft (see page 104).

2 Cover the bulgur wheat with about three times its volume
   in water, add a little salt and cook until the water is
   absorbed.

3 Chop the onions. Heat the oil in a skillet and fry the onions
   until lightly browned.

4 Stir the chestnuts and onions into the bulgur wheat. Add
   the yogurt, marjoram, and seasoning and mix thoroughly.

5 Turn the mixture into an oiled oven dish and bake in a
   moderate oven 350°F/180°C/Gas Mark 4 for about half an
   hour. Alternatively, cover with wax paper and microwave for
   about 6 minutes.

Barley with Stir-fried Garden Vegetables

THIS RECIPE USES BARLEY AS A CHANGE FROM RICE. A QUICK RECIPE.

1¹/₃ cups/¹/₂ pound/225g pot barley

Sea salt as required

3 small leeks

2 carrots

4 sticks celery

4 cups/¹/₂ pound/225g mushrooms

4 tablespoons vegetable oil

1 teaspoon ground cumin

2 tablespoons sunflower seeds

1 Cover the barley with boiling water and soak for several hours. Cook the barley in salted water until tender.

2 Slice the leeks thinly, cut the carrots into matchsticks, and chop the celery and mushrooms.

3 Heat the oil gently, add the cumin and stir well.

4 Add the vegetables to the oil and stir-fry for a few minutes until the vegetables are just tender.

5 Toast the sunflower seeds under the broiler until slightly roasted.

6 Combine the cooked barley, vegetables, and sunflower seeds, stirring well, and serve.

Big Oat Burgers

THESE ARE VERY SIMPLE TO MAKE AND USE INGREDIENTS FOUND IN MOST STORECUPBOARDS, SO THEY ARE GREAT FOR EMERGENCIES. SERVE IN BUNS WITH LETTUCE AND SLICED TOMATOES OR KETCHUP IF DESIRED. A QUICK RECIPE.

1 onion

2 cloves garlic

2 tablespoons vegetable oil plus additional as required

1 cup/4 oz/115g rolled oats

1/2 cup/2 oz/55g soy flour

2–3 tablespoons peanut butter

2 teaspoons yeast extract

1–2 teaspoons caraway seeds

4–6 tablespoons water

1 Chop the onion and garlic finely. Sauté in the oil until lightly browned.

2 In a mixing bowl combine the oats, flour, peanut butter, yeast extract, and caraway seeds. Add the onion and garlic and just enough water to form into firm patties.

3 Add just a little more oil to the skillet and fry the burgers until nicely browned on both sides.

Vegan Scottish Haggis

THIS VERY SIMPLE DISH IS PERFECT FOR A COLD WINTER'S NIGHT. SERVE WITH A VEGAN GRAVY AND BRUSSELS SPROUTS, BROCCOLI, OR SAVOY CABBAGE.

1 cup/4 oz/115g medium oatmeal

½ cup/2 oz/55g soy flour

1 cup/2 oz/55g whole-wheat bread crumbs

1 teaspoon baking powder

½ teaspoon dried mixed herbs

1 small onion

⅓ cup/3 oz/85g hard vegetable fat or shredded vegetable suet

Water as required

Sea salt as required

Freshly ground black pepper as required

1 Combine the oatmeal, soy flour, bread crumbs, baking powder, and herbs in a large mixing bowl.

2 Chop the onion finely and add to the bowl.

3 Mix in the fat (grated if not already shredded). Add enough water to make a thick pouring consistency and turn the mixture into an oiled pudding basin. Steam for two hours. Alternatively, cover with wax paper and microwave for 12 minutes. Leave for a minute or two before turning out.

Fried Cornmeal Polenta

CORNMEAL IN THE FORM OF POLENTA IS VERY POPULAR IN ITALY AND FRANCE. A QUICK RECIPE.

2 cups/^{1}/$_2$ pound/225g cornmeal
2^1/$_2$ cups/20 fl oz/570ml cold water
Pinch of sea salt
3 cups/25 fl oz/750ml boiling water
1 oz/30g vegan margarine
3 tablespoons extra virgin olive oil
Tomato sauce as required
Nutritional yeast or vegan Parmesan
   (optional)

1 Mix the cornmeal and cold water in a saucepan and add a little salt. Pour in the boiling water, then stir continuously over a low heat until beginning to boil and thicken. Place the saucepan on top of another saucepan (or use a steamer or double boiler), cover it and leave it to steam for about 30 minutes. Remove from the heat and spoon the polenta onto an oiled plate or baking sheet, smoothing it down to about ^{1}/$_2$ inch/1.5cm in depth. Cool then chill.

2 Cut the chilled polenta into squares. Heat the margarine and oil in a large skillet and fry the squares, turning them so that they are lightly browned on both sides.

3 Serve topped with a well-flavored tomato sauce and sprinkled, if desired, with nutritional yeast or vegan Parmesan.

Beans

Pulses are a mainstay of a vegan diet. High in protein and high in fiber, they are also very versatile, and there are enough different kinds to provide plenty of variety. Unlike other vegetables, beans should always be cooked until they are soft, as "al dente" beans are hard to digest.

Dried beans need to be soaked for many hours before cooking. Once soaked you should discard the soaking water, cover the beans with fresh water, bring to a boil and, simmer for the amount of time specified. (Kidney shaped beans should be vigorously boiled for 10 minutes before simmering.) Do not add salt until near the end of the cooking time as salt slows the cooking process.

Unlike fresh vegetables, beans do not lose any of their nutritional value when canned. Canned beans do tend to have a lot of salt added to them, but it is easy enough to drain and rinse them thoroughly. Buying beans in cans does, undeniably, cost considerably more than buying them dried, but you will save time by using cans.

The recipes that follow use bean quantities based on cooked rather than dried weight.

BEAN GUIDE

BUTTER BEANS *These big white beans are easy to find in the shops although canned varieties often have rather a lot o sugar added.*

LIMA BEANS *Similar to the British butter bean, though this American variety is smaller.*

NAVY (CANNELLINI) BEANS *These are little white beans, the kind found in British "baked beans". They have little of their own distinguishing flavor but for just this reason are useful in highly flavored dishes. When canned, these are usually called by their Italian name – cannellini beans. Cooking them from dried after soaking should take 45 minutes to one hour.*

GARBANZO BEANS *The taste and texture of these beans makes them a favorite around the world and they are particularly well known as the main ingredient of hummus. Cooking them from dried after soaking will take about 1½ hours.*

RED KIDNEY BEANS *The slight sweetness of these beans makes them very distinctive. Their texture is pleasing too. Cooking time after soaking should be about one hour.*

BORLOTTI (PINTO) BEANS *These brown, often speckled, kidney-shaped beans are used in the U.S. mainly for chilis. Although similar to the red kidney bean, they are less sweet and have a slightly different texture. Cooking time after soaking should be about an hour.*

ADUKI BEANS *In the Far East these are used primarily for desserts as they have a naturally sweet flavor. They are often used in macrobiotic diets. After soaking, they should be cooked for about 45 minutes.*

BLACK-EYED BEANS *These wonderfully earthy beans are much used in the deep South. After soaking, they take no more than 45 minutes of cooking. There's a secret to keeping the white part of the bean white — just add a little lemon juice to the cooking water.*

SPLIT PEAS *Both the yellow and green split peas taste similar. Once soaked, they take less than half an hour's cooking, but they can be cooked without pre-soaking. Often they are cooked to a "mush" but if the cooking time is shortened they will keep their original shape.*

BROWN AND GREEN LENTILS *Brown and green lentils are similar in flavor. They take only between 15 and 20 minutes to cook if pre-soaked, though for many dishes it is better not to pre-soak as they are then more likely to retain their texture. Without soaking, these lentils should cook for about 30 minutes.*

RED (EGYPTIAN) LENTILS *These are in fact split and hulled brown lentils. They are the easiest pulses to use, requiring no pre-soaking and only about 15 minutes cooking time.*

Lima Bean and Potato Stew

STEWS USUALLY TAKE A LONG TIME TO PREPARE, BUT IF THE BEANS AND POTATOES ARE COOKED BEFOREHAND, THIS ONE IS QUICK TO MAKE. SERVE EITHER OVER BROWN RICE OR IN A BOWL ACCOMPANIED BY WHOLE-WHEAT BREAD. A QUICK RECIPE.

$1\frac{1}{2}$ pound/680g potatoes

2 onions

2 tablespoons vegetable oil

$1\frac{1}{3}$ cups/10 fl oz/285ml vegetable
   bouillon or water

1 tablespoon finely chopped parsley

1 teaspoon dried sage

$2\frac{1}{2}$ cups/1 pound/455g or 2 cans
   (14–16 oz/400g each) cooked
   drained lima beans

1 teaspoon miso

1 Cook the potatoes in lightly salted boiling water until tender (or use leftover cooked potatoes). Drain and chop.

2 Slice the onions thinly. Sauté in the oil for a few minutes until lightly browned.

3 Stir in the bouillon or water, the parsley, and the sage. Then stir in the drained beans. Bring to a boil and simmer for 2–3 minutes.

4 Stir in the potatoes and simmer for another 2–3 minutes.

5 Remove a little of the bouillon from the saucepan and cream it with the miso in a cup before stirring it into the saucepan. Serve immediately.

Vegetable and White Bean Casserole

ALTHOUGH THIS SATISFYING, OLD-FASHIONED CASSEROLE TAKES A LONG TIME TO COOK, IT REQUIRES NO ATTENTION FOR MOST OF THAT TIME.

1½ pound/680g mixed root vegetables (carrots, turnips, rutabaga)

½ pound/225g potatoes

1 small head celery

3 onions

¼ cup/2 oz/55g vegan margarine

2½ cups/1 pound/455g or 2 cans (14–16 oz/400g each) cooked drained lima beans or navy beans

1⅓ cups/10 fl oz/285ml water

2 teaspoons yeast extract

1 can (14–16 oz/400g) tomatoes

1 cup/2 oz/55g whole-wheat bread crumbs

1 Dice the root vegetables and potatoes (peeled if desired). Trim and slice the celery and the onions.

2 Melt the margarine in a large saucepan. Add the diced vegetables, celery, and onion. Stir over a moderate heat for 5 minutes.

3 Stir in the beans, water, yeast extract, and the can of tomatoes. Bring to a boil, then transfer to a large casserole dish.

4 Cover and bake in the center of a moderate oven at 350°F/180°C/Gas Mark 4 for 1¼–1½ hours until the vegetables are cooked.

5 Remove the lid from the casserole. Sprinkle the bread crumbs over the vegetables and cook for another 20–30 minutes in the oven until the topping is crisp and golden.

Korean Kebabs (p.208)
served with basmati rice

Three Bean Salad (p.47)
and Spicy Potato Balls (p.20)

Malaysian Noodles (p.207)

No Fat Lentil and
Smoked Tofu Soup (p.4)
and Millet Salad (p.48)

Navy Bean and Root Vegetable Pie

THIS RECIPE OFFERS A PLEASANT CONTRAST OF TASTES AND TEXTURES. IT CAN BE SERVED WITH A GREEN SALAD IF DESIRED BUT IS FINE ON ITS OWN.

2 onions

1 pound/455g rutabaga

½ pound/225g carrots

2 tablespoons vegetable oil

2 tablespoons/1 oz/30g vegan margarine

¼ cup/1 oz/30g whole-wheat flour

2 cups/15 fl oz/425ml soy milk

Sea salt as required

Freshly ground black pepper as required

2½ cups/1 pound/455g or 2 cans (14–16 oz/400g each) cooked drained navy beans

2 pounds/900g mashed potatoes

1 Chop the onions. Peel and chop the rutabaga and carrots.

2 Heat the oil in a large saucepan. Add the vegetables and cover the pan, then leave to cook over a low heat until just tender – about 10–15 minutes.

3 Melt the margarine in another saucepan. Stir in the flour and then slowly add the milk, stirring constantly to avoid lumps. When it has thickened remove from the heat. Season to taste.

4 Add the drained beans to the cooked vegetables. Season to taste. Transfer the mixture to an oiled casserole dish. Spoon the white sauce over it and top with the mashed potatoes.

5 Bake at 375°F/190°C/Gas Mark 5 for 20–30 minutes, until the top has begun to turn brown. Alternatively, cover with wax paper and microwave for 6–7 minutes.

Mediterranean Beans and Chestnuts

SERVE OVER BROWN RICE OR PASTA OR AS A STEW WITH CRUSTY WHOLE-WHEAT BREAD.

4 oz/115g dried chestnuts

2 onions

3 tablespoons vegetable oil

2 cloves garlic

$^{1}/_{2}$–$^{3}/_{4}$ pound/225–340g zucchini

2 cans (14–16 oz/400g each) chopped tomatoes

2 teaspoons dried oregano

Sea salt as required

Freshly ground black pepper as required

$1^{1}/_{4}$ cups/$^{1}/_{2}$ pound/225g or 1 can (14–16 oz/400g) cooked drained navy beans

1 Soak the chestnuts in a Thermos flask until tender (see page 104).

2 Chop the onions. Heat the oil and sauté them for a minute or two while finely chopping the garlic. Add the garlic to the pan and continue cooking while chopping the zucchini; add them to the pan and continue to sauté for a few minutes longer.

3 Add the tomatoes to the pan and bring to a boil. Stir in the oregano, salt (if required – canned tomatoes can be quite salty) and pepper. Add the drained beans and chestnuts. Lower the heat and simmer, uncovered, for about 15 minutes.

Garbanzos in Spanish Sauce

THIS RECIPE MAKES A VERY PLEASANT, SPICY MIXTURE WHICH CAN BE SERVED WITH POTATOES OR OVER RICE.

1 green bell pepper

1 red bell pepper

1 fresh chili

1 onion

1 clove garlic

2 tablespoons extra virgin olive oil

1 tablespoon chopped parsley

1 pound/455g ripe tomatoes

1 teaspoon sea salt

2½ cups/1 pound/455g or 2 cans (14–16 oz/400g each) cooked drained garbanzo beans

1 Chop the bell peppers, chili, onion, garlic, and tomatoes.

2 Lightly fry the peppers, chili, onion, and garlic in the olive oil for a few minutes.

3 Add the parsley, tomatoes, and salt and cook on a low heat for about half an hour, stirring occasionally, until the tomatoes are pulped.

4 Add the cooked garbanzo beans, heat through and serve.

Garbanzo and Eggplant Ragout

THIS DISH COMES FROM GREECE WHERE FOOD IS GENERALLY SERVED LUKEWARM. OF COURSE, IT COULD BE SERVED EITHER HOT OR COLD INSTEAD, BUT THERE ARE TIMES WHEN IT IS QUITE HANDY TO HAVE A DISH THAT CAN BE LEFT ON THE TABLE FOR PEOPLE TO HELP THEMSELVES TO, WITHOUT WORRYING ABOUT KEEPING IT EITHER HOT OR REFRIGERATED.

1 large eggplant

2 large onions

$^1/_2$ cup/4 fl oz/125ml extra virgin
   olive oil

$2^1/_2$ cups/1 pound/455g or 2 cans
   (14–16 oz/400g each) garbanzo
   beans

2 cans (14–16 oz/400g each) tomatoes

1 teaspoon dried mint

Sea salt as required

Freshly ground black pepper
   as required

1 Chop the eggplant into cubes and chop the onions coarsely. Heat the olive oil gently and sauté the eggplant and onion until tenderized. Add the cooked garbanzo beans, canned tomatoes, mint, and seasoning.

2 Cook uncovered, over a low heat, for half an hour.

3 Cool and serve at room temperature.

Garbanzo Stroganoff

THIS IS A REALLY TASTY DISH AND AN ALL-TIME FAVORITE. A QUICK RECIPE.

1 onion

4 cups/½ pound/225g mushrooms

2 tablespoons/1 oz/30g vegan
  margarine

4 tablespoons vegetable bouillon or
  water

¼ teaspoon freshly ground nutmeg

1 teaspoon soy sauce

¼ teaspoon mustard powder

2½ cups/1 pound/455g or 2 cans
  (14–16 oz/400g each) cooked
  drained garbanzo beans

2 teaspoons cider vinegar or wine
  vinegar

2 cups/10 oz/285g whole-wheat
  noodles

¾ cup/7 fl oz/200ml soy yogurt

1 Chop the onion and mushrooms. Melt the margarine and
   sauté the vegetables until soft.

2 Add the bouillon, seasonings, garbanzo beans, and vinegar.
   Cover and simmer on a low heat for about 10 minutes.

3 Meanwhile, cook the noodles for 10–15 minutes until soft.

4 Add the yogurt to the garbanzo bean mixture over the
   lowest possible heat, stirring constantly without bringing to
   a boil, until heated through.

5 Serve over the cooked noodles.

Garbanzo and Sesame Roast with Tomato Topping

SERVE THIS ROAST WITH SEASONAL VEGETABLES AND POTATOES.

ROAST

2 onions

2 tablespoons vegetable oil

1 large or 2 small carrots

$^{1}/_{6}$ cup/1 oz/30g sesame seeds

$2^{1}/_{2}$ cups/1 pound/455g or 2 cans
   (14–16 oz/400g each) cooked
   drained garbanzo beans

2 tablespoons water

1 tablespoon chick pea flour

$^{1}/_{3}$ cup/2 oz/55g tahini

1 teaspoon dried or 2 teaspoons fresh
   marjoram

TOPPING

$1^{1}/_{2}$ tablespoons vegan margarine

2 tablespoons whole-wheat flour

$1^{1}/_{3}$ cups/10 fl oz/285ml soy milk

$^{1}/_{4}$ cup/2 oz/55g tomato paste

1 teaspoon dried basil

Sea salt as required

Freshly ground black pepper
   as required

4 tablespoons nutritional yeast

1 Chop the onions and sauté them in the vegetable oil in a
   large saucepan for a few minutes until tenderized.

2 Grate the carrots finely. Set aside. Toast the sesame seeds
   until lightly browned, cool slightly and grind in a food
   processor. Set aside.

3 Remove the pan from the heat and add the beans (drained)
   to the pan, mashing them coarsely.

4 Put the water in a small cup and beat in the chick pea flour
   with a fork. Add this to the bean mixture. Stir in the tahini,
   carrots, marjoram, and ground sesame seeds.

5 Turn the mixture into an oiled pan and bake at
   350°F/180°C/Gas Mark 4.

6 Meanwhile, make the topping. Melt the margarine in a
   small pan and stir in the flour. Gradually stir in the milk and
   the tomato paste, stirring constantly until thickened. Stir in
   the basil and seasoning. Remove from the heat and stir in
   the yeast.

7 When the roast has been in the oven for about half an hour
   take it out and spoon the topping over it. Return it to the
   oven and bake for about another 15 minutes.

"Hummus" Patties

SERVE THESE UNUSUAL RISSOLES WITH A GREEN SALAD FOR A LIGHT LUNCH OR DINNER, OR WITH POTATOES AND VEGETABLES FOR A MORE FILLING MEAL. A QUICK RECIPE.

2½ cups/1 pound/455g or 2 cans
    (14–16 oz/400g each) cooked
    drained garbanzo beans
2 cloves garlic
2 cups/4 oz/115g whole-wheat
    bread crumbs
3 tablespoons tahini
2 teaspoons ground cumin seeds
Juice of ½ lemon (optional)
Vegetable oil as required

1 Put the drained beans in a large mixing bowl and mash them well. Mince the garlic and add it to the bowl.
2 Add the bread crumbs, tahini, cumin seeds, and lemon juice if using (the taste and texture will be fine without it). Add seasoning if desired. Mix well and form into eight large or 16 small patties.
3 Heat some oil in a skillet and shallow-fry the patties until lightly browned on both sides.

Lentil and Rice Loaf

SERVE THIS WITH SEASONAL VEGETABLES.

1¹/₃ cups/¹/₂ pound/225g brown rice

1 cup/6 oz/170g red lentils

1 small onion

1 tablespoon vegetable oil

1 tablespoon whole-wheat flour

3 tablespoons soy milk

¹/₂ teaspoon dried sage

¹/₂ cup/2 oz/55g walnuts

Sea salt as required

1 Cook the rice until very tender.

2 Cover the lentils with salted water and cook until very tender. Mash well.

3 Chop the onion finely and sauté it in the oil until tender. Add the flour and stir well. Now pour in the milk, stirring constantly.

4 Chop the walnuts and add these to the saucepan together with the cooked rice, cooked lentils, and sage. Mix together well.

5 Pack into an oiled bread pan and bake in a moderate oven at 350°F/180°C/Gas Mark 4 for 30–40 minutes until slightly browned on top. Alternatively, cover with wax paper and microwave for 7–8 minutes.

Masoor Dahl

DAHL IS THE GENERIC TERM FOR PULSE DISHES IN INDIA. RED LENTILS ARE THE EASIEST KIND TO FIND AND COOK. DAHL IS USUALLY SERVED AS A SIDE DISH, AND THIS COULD CERTAINLY BE SERVED AS JUST PART OF A LARGE MEAL, BUT IF SERVED OVER RICE IT IS SUBSTANTIAL ENOUGH AS A MEAL IN ITSELF. A QUICK RECIPE.

$1^{1}/_{2}$ cups/9 oz/255g red lentils

2 teaspoons cumin seeds

Sea salt as required

$^{1}/_{2}$ teaspoon turmeric

Pinch of cayenne pepper

$^{1}/_{2}$ pound/225g tomatoes

$^{3}/_{4}$ pound/340g potatoes

4 cups/35 fl oz/1 litre water

2 onions

4 cloves garlic

$^{1}/_{4}$ cup/2 oz/55g vegan margarine

1 Rinse the lentils and place them in a saucepan. Grind the cumin seeds and add them to the pan, along with the salt, turmeric, and cayenne.

2 Chop the tomatoes and potatoes into fairly small pieces. Add them to the pan. Pour the water over, cover, bring to a boil, then lower the heat and simmer for about half an hour.

3 Slice the onions thinly. Chop the garlic finely. Heat the margarine in a skillet and add the onions and garlic. Fry until golden brown.

4 Stir the contents of the skillet into the lentil mixture and serve.

Lentil Burgers

THESE ARE NICE "MEATY" BURGERS WHICH CAN BE SERVED IN A BUN WITH THE USUAL BURGER
TRIMMINGS OR WITH GRAVY AND VEGETABLES AS A MAIN COURSE.

1⅓ cups/½ pound/225g brown lentils

5 cups/40 fl oz/1120ml water

⅔ cup/4 oz/115g bulgur wheat

Sea salt as required

2 teaspoons yeast extract

2 teaspoons tomato paste

2 onions

4 cups/½ pound/225g mushrooms

Whole-wheat flour as required

3 tablespoons vegetable oil plus
   additional as required

1 Cover the lentils with boiling water and leave to soak for
   several hours. Drain.

2 Put the lentils into a small saucepan, cover with the water,
   bring to a boil, lower the heat, cover and leave to simmer for
   about 15 minutes.

3 Add the bulgur wheat and a little salt, and continue cooking
   for another 10 minutes or so, until the lentils and wheat are
   tender and all the water has been absorbed.

4 Stir in the yeast extract and tomato paste.

5 Chop the onion and mushrooms finely. Sauté in the oil until
   tender. Stir into the lentil mixture.

6 Leave the mixture to cool, then form into four burgers. Coat
   each side in a little whole-wheat flour, then fry in vegetable
   oil until browned on both sides.

Megedarra

THIS IS A VARIATION OF A TRADITIONAL MIDDLE-EASTERN DISH. IT WOULD BE VEGAN IN ITS NATIVE HABITAT WERE IT NOT FOR THE YOGURT TOPPING, BUT IN MY OPINION THE YOGURT REALLY MAKES THE DISH.

1³⁄₄ cups/10 oz/285g brown rice
1³⁄₄ cups/10 oz/285g brown lentils
Sea salt as required
Vegetable oil as required
3 large onions
Freshly ground black pepper
   as required
Soy yogurt as required

1 Put the rice and lentils in a large saucepan, pour boiling water over them, cover the pan and leave to soak for several hours.

2 Chop one of the onions finely and fry in a little oil until tenderized and turning golden.

3 Drain the rice and lentils then return them to the saucepan, cover with fresh water, add the fried onion and a little sea salt, and bring to a boil. Lower the heat and leave to cook until tender – about 25 minutes. Taste, and add a little more if necessary. Grind in pepper to taste.

4 A few minutes before the rice and lentils are ready slice the other two onions thinly and fry them in very hot oil, stirring constantly so they don't burn but turn very dark brown.

5 Put the sliced fried onions on top of the rice and lentil mixture. Spoon yogurt over the dish while eating it.

Lentil Pastichio

PASTICHIO IS A GREEK DISH OF MACARONI AND MINCED MEAT. THIS IS A VEGAN VERSION USING BROWN LENTILS INSTEAD.

1$\frac{1}{3}$ cups/$\frac{1}{2}$ pound/225g brown lentils

4 tablespoons vegan margarine

1 large onion

2 cloves garlic

1 small green bell pepper

2 cups/4 oz/115g mushrooms

1 can (14–16 oz/400g) tomatoes

2 teaspoons dried oregano

2 teaspoons ground cinnamon

2 cups/$\frac{1}{2}$ pound/225g whole-wheat
   macaroni

$\frac{1}{4}$ cup/1 oz/30g whole-wheat flour

1$\frac{1}{3}$ cups/10 fl oz/285ml soy milk

Sea salt as required

Freshly ground black pepper
   as required

$\frac{1}{4}$ cup/1 oz/30g nutritional yeast

1 Rinse the lentils, cover with water and add a little salt. Bring to a boil, then lower the heat and simmer, covered.

2 Melt 2 tablespoons of the margarine in a large saucepan. Chop the onion and sauté it for a few minutes until it begins to soften. Meanwhile, mince the garlic and chop the bell pepper and mushrooms. Add these ingredients to the saucepan, together with the tomatoes, oregano, and cinnamon. Bring to a boil, then lower the heat and leave to simmer.

3 Cook the macaroni until just tender.

4 After the tomato mixture has been simmering for about 10 minutes – by which time the lentils should have been simmering for about 20 minutes – spoon the lentils into the larger pan and let the whole lot simmer together for a few more minutes.

5 Melt the remaining 2 tablespoons margarine in another saucepan. Sprinkle in the flour, then slowly stir in the milk to make a white sauce. Season well, remove from the heat and stir in the yeast.

6 Oil a large casserole dish. Put the cooked and drained macaroni on the bottom. Place a layer of the lentil mixture over the pasta. Finally, spoon the sauce over the top. Bake at 400°F/200°C/Gas Mark 6 for about half an hour.

Adzuki and Vegetable Pie

ADZUKI BEANS DO NOT TAKE TOO LONG TO COOK AND ARE COMBINED HERE WITH OTHER INTERESTING INGREDIENTS IN A PIE.

1 cup/½ pound/225g adzuki beans

1 onion

2 leeks

2 carrots

2 small rutabagas

1 sour apple

½ cup/3 oz/85g currants

⅔ cup/3 oz/85g walnuts

2 tablespoons vegetable oil

Sea salt as required

Pinch of ground cinnamon

1 quantity Whole-wheat Pastry (see page 65)

1 Cover the adzuki beans with boiling water and leave to soak for several hours or overnight. Drain, cover with fresh water and cook until tender.

2 Chop the onion, leeks, carrots, rutabagas, and apple. Chop the walnuts separately.

3 Sauté the vegetables in the oil until tender.

4 Combine the cooked adzuki beans, sautéed vegetables, currants, chopped walnuts, salt, and cinnamon.

5 Line a pie dish with the pastry – all of it or, if preferred, save some to make strips across the top. Fill with the bean and vegetable mixture.

6 Bake in a moderately hot oven at 375°F/190°C/Gas Mark 5 for about half an hour, until the pastry is golden brown.

Armenian Black-eyed Peas and Nuts

THIS IS A BLACK-EYED PEA DISH FROM THE EAST.

1¼ cups/½ pound/225g black-eyed
   peas
2 onions
½ cup/4 fl oz/125ml olive oil
1 teaspoon raw cane sugar
1 teaspoon sea salt
1 can (8 oz/225g) tomatoes
2 teaspoons tomato paste
1 cup/5 oz/140g mixed nuts
1 tablespoon chopped parsley

1 Cover the black-eyed peas with boiling water and leave
   to soak for several hours or overnight. Cook until tender
   and drain.
2 Chop the onions and sauté them in the olive oil until soft.
   Chop the nuts coarsely.
3 Liquidize the tomatoes and add them to the saucepan with
   the rest of the ingredients.
4 Simmer for 10–15 minutes before serving.

Chili Bean Roast with Tomato Sauce

SERVE WITH A SEASONAL GREEN VEGETABLE AND BOILED OR BAKED POTATOES.

2 onions

1 small green bell pepper

3 cloves garlic

4 tablespoons vegetable oil

2 teaspoons ground cumin

1 teaspoon dried oregano

$^{1}/_{2}$ teaspoon (or to taste) chili powder

$2^{1}/_{2}$ cups/1 pound/225g or 2 cans
   (14–16 oz/400g each) cooked
   drained pinto beans

2 cups/4 oz/115g whole-wheat
   bread crumbs

$^{1}/_{4}$ cup/1 oz/30g whole-wheat flour

2 cups/15 fl oz/425ml water

3 tablespoons tomato paste

Few drops Tabasco sauce

Sea salt as required

Freshly ground black pepper
   as required

1 Chop the onions and bell pepper finely. Mince the garlic. Heat 2 tablespoons of the oil in a skillet and sauté these ingredients until they begin to brown. Stir in the cumin, oregano, and chili powder and cook for a minute or two longer. Remove from heat.

2 Mash the drained beans in a bowl. Add the bread crumbs and the contents of the skillet and mix well. Turn the mixture into a baking dish and bake at 350°F/180°C/Gas Mark 4 for about half an hour. Alternatively, cover with wax paper and microwave for 7–8 minutes.

3 To make the sauce, heat the remaining 2 tablespoons oil and stir in the flour. Add the water slowly, stirring constantly to avoid lumps. Stir in the tomato paste and Tabasco sauce. When the mixture is thick and boiling season to taste.

Nuts

Nuts are high in protein and high in health-promoting fats and oils. They're a must if you're following a vegan diet – and a delight whatever your diet. They are undoubtedly high in calories, but the calories in nuts are not empty. Nuts are a terrifically healthy source of energy and eaten in the right proportions will not lead to weight gain.

NUT GUIDE

ALMONDS Unblanched almonds have the most interesting flavor although blanched almonds tend to be more useful for cooking. Really fresh almonds will be crunchy, and have a hint of sweetness, but the flavor of almonds is best brought out by toasting them on the broiler.

BRAZIL NUTS These are the richest of nuts – and their nutritional benefits are increasingly highly regarded. They're difficult to grind in a liquidizer as their rich oil content tends to make the mix soft and gummy. You can solve this problem and use ground brazils in your cooking by adding a slice of bread to the mix and using a blend of bread crumbs and ground nut.

WALNUTS Fresh walnuts out of the shell are often tastier than those bought ready-shelled, which can be bitter. If you're buying pre-shelled walnuts it's best to opt for halves instead of chopped pieces as these will tend to be fresher. As a rule, the paler the nuts, the better the flavor will be.

PECAN NUTS An exquisite flavor, similar to the walnut, pecans are often the most expensive nut in the shop. With a sweet taste that's brought out even more by lightly toasting, pecans are perfect for dessert dishes as well as savory.

PEANUTS *By botanical definition, peanuts are not really nuts at all – but they look like nuts, and have a very similar nutritional composition to the other "true" nuts so their differences are usually overlooked. They can be used raw from the shell or roasted and famously can be used to make peanut butter.*

CASHEW NUTS *Another nut that's not a true nut, cashews can be used to make a useful vegan "cream". With a light, delicate taste and slightly softer texture than many other nuts, they make an interesting addition to many dishes. Although it's cheaper to buy chopped or broken cashews, whole nuts do retain the better flavor.*

CHESTNUTS *Again not a true nut, the chestnut is actually a starch and is nutritionally quite different from the other nuts in this list. Lower in calories and without the high protein content of a true nut, chestnuts are still a key ingredient in vegan cooking. Chestnuts can be bought fresh, canned or dried. Dried chestnuts can be soaked and cooked until soft, but the best way of preparing them is to soak them in boiling water in a wide-rimmed Thermos flask until they are tender. Leave them for at least 12 hours, and preferably longer, and they should come out ready for use.*

Celebration Nut Roast

THE FLAVOR OF GROUND HAZELNUTS TOGETHER WITH THE TEXTURE OF CASHEWS IS AN UNBEATABLE COMBINATION IN THIS "SPECIAL OCCASION" ROAST. SERVE IT WITH GRAVY AND SEASONAL VEGETABLES.

1 onion

3 tablespoons vegetable oil

2 small tomatoes

¼ cup/1 oz/30g whole-wheat flour

⅔ cup/5 fl oz/140ml water

1 tablespoon soy sauce

¾ cup/4 oz/115g hazelnuts

¾ cup/4 oz/115g broken cashew nuts

1½ cups/3 oz/85g whole-wheat
    bread crumbs

1 teaspoon dried mixed herbs

¼ cup/1 oz/30g soy flour

1 Chop the onion finely and sauté it in the oil until tender.

2 Peel and chop the tomatoes and add them to the pan. Cook for 5 minutes.

3 Stir in the flour and slowly add the water, stirring constantly to avoid lumps. Remove from the heat.

4 Grind the hazelnuts and add them to the sauce together with all the other ingredients. Mix very thoroughly and place in a bread pan or pie dish.

5 Bake in a moderate oven at 350°F/180°C/Gas Mark 4 for 45 minutes–1 hour.

Hazelnut and Potato Bake

SERVE THIS TASTY DISH WITH A GREEN SALAD.

1$^1/_3$ cups/6 oz/170g hazelnuts

2 sticks celery

3 scallions

1 teaspoon garlic salt

1$^1/_2$ cups/$^3/_4$ pound/340g mashed
potatoes

2 tablespoons/1 oz/30g vegan
margarine

$^1/_4$ cup/1 oz/30g whole-wheat flour

$^2/_3$ cup/5 fl oz/140ml soy milk

1 Grind the nuts and chop the celery and scallions finely.

2 Combine these ingredients with the mashed potatoes and garlic salt.

3 Melt the margarine in a small saucepan and stir in the flour. Slowly add the milk, stirring constantly to avoid lumps. When boiling and thickened, combine this sauce with the mashed potato and nut mixture.

4 Place the mixture in a baking dish and bake in a moderate oven at 350°F/180°C/Gas Mark 4 for about half an hour. Alternatively, cover with wax paper and microwave for 6–7 minutes.

Cashew Rice Roast

THIS IS A SIMPLE, EFFECTIVE MAIN DISH, WHICH SHOULD BE SERVED WITH VEGETABLE ACCOMPANIMENTS.

$^3/_4$ cup/4 oz/115g brown rice

$1^2/_3$ cups/$^1/_2$ pound/225g cashews

1 onion

2 cloves garlic

4 tablespoons vegetable oil

2 cups/4 oz/115g whole-wheat
   bread crumbs

2 teaspoons yeast extract

1 teaspoon dried mixed herbs

Sea salt as required

Freshly ground black pepper
   as required

1 Cook the rice until tender (or use leftover cooked rice) and grind the cashew nuts.

2 Chop the onion and garlic finely and sauté them in the vegetable oil until browned.

3 Combine all the ingredients and press the mixture into a loaf pan.

4 Bake for about half an hour in a moderate oven at 350°F/180°C/Gas Mark 4.

Cashew-stuffed Eggplant

THIS IS AN UNUSUAL FILLING FOR EGGPLANTS BUT A VERY PLEASING ONE. SERVE WITH SEASONAL VEGETABLES AND POTATOES.

2 large or 4 small eggplants
1 pound/455g onions
1²/₃ cups/½ pound/225g cashews
2 teaspoons yeast extract

1 Cut the tops off the eggplants and simmer them in boiling water for half an hour. Set them aside to drain and cool.

2 Chop the onions finely and cook them in enough water to cover, along with the yeast extract, until tender. Drain the surplus liquid.

3 Grind the cashews and mix them with the cooked onion.

4 Slice the eggplants in half, scoop out the flesh from the centers, finely chop and add to the cashew–onion mixture.

5 Pile the mixture into the eggplant halves and bake in a fairly hot oven at 400°F/200°C/Gas Mark 6 for 20 minutes.

Continental Stuffed Eggplants

THIS IS AN ELABORATE STUFFED EGGPLANT DISH WITH A MEDITERRANEAN FLAVOR.

2 large or 4 small eggplants

1 clove garlic

1 onion

2 large tomatoes

²/₃ cup/3 oz/85g almonds, brazils, or hazelnuts

4 tablespoons rolled oats

4 tablespoons vegetable oil

2 tablespoons whole-wheat flour

1 can (14–16 oz/400g) tomatoes

1 teaspoon dried basil or marjoram

Sea salt as required

Freshly ground black pepper as required

1 Cut the tops off the eggplants and place them in boiling water for 5–10 minutes.

2 Set aside to drain, then slice them in half and scoop out the flesh, leaving the skins intact.

3 Chop the garlic finely. Chop the onion, the 2 large tomatoes, and the eggplant flesh.

4 Sauté the above ingredients in half the oil for a few minutes.

5 Grind the nuts and add them to the saucepan together with the oats, stirring well.

6 Fill the eggplant skins with this mixture and bake them in a moderately hot oven at 375°F/190°C/Gas Mark 5 for about half an hour.

7 Meanwhile, heat the rest of the oil in a small saucepan and stir in the flour. Remove from the heat.

8 Pour the whole can of tomatoes into the liquidizer and blend them thoroughly. Add this to the saucepan, mixing well. Return to the heat, stirring constantly to avoid lumps. When thickened and boiling, add the herbs and seasoning to taste.

9 Pour the tomato sauce over the eggplants when ready to serve.

Bite-sized All-nut Croquettes

THESE LITTLE CROQUETTES ARE GREAT SERVED AT PARTIES, WHERE THEY ARE ALWAYS VERY POPULAR. THEY CAN BE SERVED HOT OR COLD AND CAN BE MADE INTO LARGER CROQUETTES FOR SERVING AS PART OF A MEAL.

$1^{2}/_{3}$ cups/$^{1}/_{2}$ pound/225g mixed nuts

1 small onion

2 tablespoons/1 oz/30g vegan
   margarine

$^{1}/_{2}$ cup/2 oz/55g whole-wheat flour

$1^{1}/_{3}$ cups/10 fl oz/285ml soy milk

1 teaspoon lemon juice

1 teaspoon dried mixed herbs

Sea salt as required

Freshly ground black pepper
   as required

Vegetable oil for frying as required

1 Chop the nuts very finely and grate the onion.

2 Melt the fat, stir in the flour, then add the milk, stirring constantly to avoid lumps.

3 When thickened, add all the other ingredients, seasoning to taste.

4 Leave the mixture to cool, then form into small croquette shapes or, if you prefer, balls.

5 Deep fry them in hot oil until brown.

Steam-cooked Nut Loaf

THIS MAKES A PLEASANT CHANGE FROM A NUT ROAST — IT HAS A SIMILAR FLAVOR BUT A COMPLETELY DIFFERENT TEXTURE. SERVE WITH SEASONAL VEGETABLES AND GRAVY IF DESIRED.

2 onions

2 tablespoons vegetable oil

2 tablespoons whole-wheat flour

$^2/_3$ cup/5 fl oz/140ml water

2 teaspoons yeast extract

$1^1/_3$ cups/6 oz/170g brazil nuts

$^1/_2$ cup/2 oz/55g broken cashews

3 tablespoons soy flour

115g/4 oz/2 cups whole-wheat bread crumbs

1 teaspoon dried thyme

1 Chop the onions finely and sauté them in the oil until brown.

2 Add the flour. Slowly add the water, stirring constantly to avoid lumps, and then add the yeast extract. When the sauce has boiled and thickened, remove the pan from the heat.

3 Grind the brazils and add them to the mixture together with the broken cashews, soy flour, bread crumbs, and thyme. Mix well.

4 Turn into a pudding basin, cover with aluminum foil, and steam for $1^1/_2$–2 hours. Alternatively, cover with wax paper and microwave for 7–8 minutes; leave for a minute or two before turning out.

Crunchy Nuts and Mushroom Cream

THIS KIND OF DISH, SOMETIMES CALLED A "CROUSTADE" IS ALWAYS POPULAR. SERVE IT WITH SEASONAL VEGETABLES AND POTATOES. SUITABLE FOR A DINNER PARTY.

1 cup/4 oz/115g whole-wheat bread crumbs

1/2 cup/2 oz/55g ground almonds

1–2 cloves garlic

1/2 cup/4 oz/115g vegan margarine

1 teaspoon dried mixed herbs

1 cup/4 oz/115g chopped almonds

6 cups/12 oz/340g mushrooms

1/4 cup/1 oz/30g whole-wheat flour

2/3 cup/5 fl oz/140ml soy milk

2 tomatoes

Sea salt as required

Freshly ground black pepper as required

Grated nutmeg as required

1 Combine the crumbs and ground almonds. Rub half the margarine into this mixture, then stir in the mixed herbs, chopped almonds, and minced garlic.

2 Turn the mixture into an oiled ovenproof dish. Press down firmly and bake in a hot oven at 425°F/220°C/Gas Mark 7 until lightly browned and crisp.

3 Slice the mushrooms and sauté them in the remainder of the margarine until tender.

4 Add the flour and stir well. Then add the milk slowly, stirring constantly to avoid lumps. Bring to a boil and simmer for 2 minutes. Season to taste.

5 Spoon the mixture on top of the bread crumb-and-nut base and spread evenly.

6 Slice the tomatoes and arrange them on the top.

7 Return dish to the oven for 10–15 minutes and serve hot.

Almond and Vegetable Curry

GROUND ALMONDS WORK WELL IN A CURRY, MAKING IT RICH AND CREAMY. TO MAKE IT QUICKER YOU COULD USE GROUND SPICES INSTEAD OF GRINDING WHOLE ONES, OR EVEN USE CURRY POWDER, BUT IT WON'T TASTE AS NICE. SERVE THE CURRY OVER BROWN RICE, WITH MANGO CHUTNEY.

½ cup/2 oz/55g slivered almonds

2 onions

1 clove garlic

2 tablespoons/1 oz/30g vegan margarine

2 teaspoons cumin seeds

2 teaspoons coriander seeds

8 cloves

½ teaspoon ground cinnamon

½ teaspoon turmeric

¼ teaspoon chili powder (or to taste)

Sea salt as required

Freshly ground black pepper as required

2½ cups/20 fl oz/570ml water

1 tablespoon tomato paste

1½ pound/680g mixed vegetables (fresh or frozen)

1 cup/4 oz/115g ground almonds

1 Toast the slivered almonds under the broiler until very lightly browned, then set aside.

2 Chop the onions. Mince the garlic. Heat the margarine in a large saucepan and fry the onions and garlic for a few minutes until the onions begin to change color.

3 If using fresh vegetables, chop them quite small, grading them in size so that whatever takes longest to cook is the smallest. (Frozen vegetables can be used straight from the freezer.)

4 Grind the cumin and coriander seeds and the cloves. Add to the saucepan, together with the other spices and seasonings. Continue frying for a minute or two longer, then pour in the water and add the tomato paste.

5 Add the vegetables to the saucepan. When the mixture is boiling, lower the heat, cover, and simmer for a few minutes until the vegetables are nearly done.

6 Stir in the ground almonds and cook for a few minutes longer. Sprinkle the toasted almonds over the top before serving.

Brazil Nut Moussaka

USING BRAZIL NUTS IN PLACE OF GROUND MEAT IN MOUSSAKA GIVES AN UNUSUAL AND PLEASING RESULT. SERVE THIS DISH WITH A GREEN SALAD.

1½ pound/680g eggplants

Sea salt as required

2 onions

8 tablespoons/4 oz/115g vegetable oil

1½ cups/½ pound/225g brazil nuts

2 cups/4 oz/115g bread crumbs

3 tablespoons tomato paste

1⅓ cups/10 fl oz/285ml water

2 teaspoons yeast extract

1 teaspoon ground cinnamon

2 tablespoons/1 oz/30g vegan
  margarine

2 tablespoons whole-wheat flour

3 cups/25 fl oz/750ml soy milk

Sea salt as required

Freshly ground black pepper
  as required

Grating nutmeg

1 Slice the eggplants thinly, salt them, put them in a colander with a weight on them, and leave them for at least half an hour.

2 Chop the onions. Heat half the oil in a saucepan and sauté the onions for a few minutes.

3 Grind the nuts. Add them to the saucepan, along with the bread crumbs, water, yeast extract, and cinnamon. Bring to a boil, then lower the heat and simmer for a few minutes.

4 Rinse the eggplant slices, drain on paper towels and squeeze gently. Heat the other half of the oil in a skillet and fry the slices gently (it may be necessary to do them in batches), turning them once. Drain well.

5 Heat the margarine in a saucepan, then stir in the flour. Add the milk very gradually, stirring constantly, and bring to a boil. Season with salt, pepper, and nutmeg.

6 Place the eggplant slices and the nutmeg mixture in layers in a casserole dish, starting and ending with eggplant. Pour the sauce over the top.

7 Bake at 375°F/190°C/Gas Mark 5 for about half an hour. Alternatively, cover with wax paper and microwave for 6–7 minutes.

Spinach and Almond Roast

SERVE THIS ROAST WITH VEGETABLES — A MIXTURE OF CAULIFLOWER, CARROT, AND PEAS GOES WELL.

3/4–1 pound/340–455g spinach

1 onion

1 clove garlic

2 tablespoons vegetable oil

2 cups/1/2 pound/225g ground almonds

1 1/2 cups/3 oz/85g whole-wheat bread
   crumbs

2 tablespoons tomato paste

1 tablespoon soy sauce

1 teaspoon dried marjoram

Sea salt as required

Freshly ground black pepper
   as required

1 Wash and chop the spinach. Steam it for a few minutes until just tender.

2 Chop the onion and garlic finely. Fry them in the oil for a few minutes until just beginning to brown.

3 Combine all the ingredients and place them in a baking dish or, if you prefer, a loaf pan. Bake at 350°F/180°C/Gas Mark 4 for about half an hour.

Spicy Rice and Walnut Roast

THIS RECIPE IS A WAY OF USING LEFTOVER RICE IN A ROAST INSTEAD OF STIR-FRYING IT.

1½ cups/½ pound/225g brown rice

2 onions

2 cloves garlic

2 tablespoons vegetable oil

6 oz/170g walnuts

1 cup/2 oz/55g whole-wheat bread
   crumbs

2 teaspoons curry powder

Sea salt as required

Freshly ground black pepper
   as required

1 cup/8 fl oz/225ml soy yogurt

1 Cook the rice (or remove previously cooked rice from the
   refrigerator).

2 Chop the onions and garlic finely. Sauté them in the oil for a
   few minutes in a large saucepan. Remove from heat.

3 Grind the walnuts. Add them to the pan together with the
   rice, bread crumbs, curry powder, seasoning, and yogurt.
   Stir well and turn into a casserole dish.

4 Bake at 350°F/180°C/Gas Mark 4 for about half an hour.
   Alternatively, cover with wax paper and microwave for
   7–8 minutes.

Cornmeal and Walnut Squares with a Thick Soy Sauce

THIS REQUIRES ADVANCE PREPARATION BUT TAKES ONLY MINUTES AT MEAL TIME. SERVE THE SQUARES WITH THE SAUCE AND SEASONAL VEGETABLES.

FOR THE SQUARES

2 onions

2 tablespoons vegetable oil plus
   additional for frying

1¹/₃ cups/6 oz/170g cornmeal

1¹/₃ cups/6 oz/170g whole-wheat flour

1¹/₃ cups/6 oz/170g chopped walnuts

3³/₄ cups/30 fl oz/850ml hot water

2–3 tablespoons soy sauce

FOR THE SAUCE

2¹/₂ cups/20 fl oz/570ml water

¹/₂ cup/2 oz/55g whole-wheat flour

2–3 tablespoons soy sauce

1 Chop the onions finely. Heat the oil in a heavy-bottomed saucepan and fry the onions until they begin to brown. Stir in the cornmeal and flour and continue to stir over a medium heat for several minutes.

2 Add the nuts, hot water, and soy sauce, stirring constantly. Lower the heat and continue stirring until it is thick and smooth. Transfer the mixture to an oiled baking sheet and smooth to about 1 inch/2.5cm thick. Leave to cool then refrigerate.

3 To make the sauce put the water, flour, and soy sauce in a liquidizer and blend. Pour the mixture into a saucepan and heat gently, stirring constantly to avoid lumps. When the mixture is boiling, lower the heat to minimum and let it simmer for a few minutes until it no longer has any "raw" taste.

4 Cut the nut mixture into squares and shallow-fry the squares until they are well browned on both sides.

Chestnut Stew

THIS STEW CAN BE SERVED OVER BROWN RICE, OR WITH POTATOES OR BREAD.

2 onions

4 tomatoes

3 cups/6 oz/170g mushrooms

2 tablespoons vegetable oil

Freshly ground black pepper as
   required

²/₃ cup/5 fl oz/140ml water

6 oz/170g dried chestnuts soaked in a
   wide-rimmed Thermos flask until
   tender (see page 104)

2 teaspoons yeast extract

2 tablespoons chopped parsley

1 Chop the onions. Peel the tomatoes; set two aside and chop
   the other two. Chop the mushrooms.

2 Heat the oil in a large saucepan. Sauté the onions, chopped
   tomatoes, and mushrooms for a few minutes. Grind pepper
   into the mixture. Add the water and chestnuts. Bring to a
   boil, then lower the heat and simmer, uncovered, for
   10–15 minutes.

3 Check the stew and if it is dry add a little more water; if
   there is too much liquid raise the heat (the amount of liquid
   will depend on size and juiciness of the tomatoes).

4 Slice the remaining tomatoes and place them under a broiler
   until tender.

5 Stir the yeast extract into the stew. Serve it topped with the
   slices of broiled tomato and the parsley.

Chestnut and Mushroom Pie

THIS IS A DELICIOUS COMBINATION OF TASTES AND TEXTURES. SERVE IT WITH SEASONAL VEGETABLES FOR A SPECIAL OCCASION. SUITABLE FOR A DINNER PARTY.

2 onions

3 tablespoons vegetable oil

6 cups/¾ pound/340g mushrooms

½ cup/2 oz/55g whole-wheat flour

2 cups/15 fl oz/425ml vegetable bouillon or water

2 tablespoons soy sauce

Sea salt as required

Freshly ground black pepper as required

¼ teaspoon freshly ground nutmeg

½ pound/225g dried chestnuts soaked in a wide-rimmed Thermos flask until tender (see page 104)

1 quantity Whole-wheat Pastry (see page 65)

1 Chop the onions and sauté them in the oil in a saucepan for a few minutes until they begin to brown. Slice the mushrooms, add them to the pan and cook for a few minutes until they are tenderized.

2 Sprinkle the flour over the vegetables and stir well. Slowly pour over the bouillon or water, stirring constantly. Bring to a boil, lower the heat, and simmer. Season with soy sauce, salt, pepper, and nutmeg. Stir in the chestnuts and let the mixture cool a little.

3 Roll out the pastry and line the bottom and sides of a pie dish with about two-thirds of it. Put in the chestnut and mushroom mixture and top with the rest of the pastry. Prick with a fork, then bake at 400°F/200°C/Gas Mark 6 for about half an hour.

Chestnut Roast

THIS WOULD BE A GOOD CHRISTMAS DISH, PARTICULARLY WITH A MISO GRAVY POURED OVER IT.

½ pound/225g dried chestnuts which have been soaked in a Thermos flask (see page 104)

2 onions

3 tablespoons vegetable oil

2 cups/4 oz/115g whole-wheat bread crumbs

2 tablespoons soy sauce

2 tablespoons soy flour

1 cup/8 fl oz/225ml water

1 teaspoon dried sage

½ teaspoon dried thyme

Sea salt as required

Freshly ground black pepper as required

1 Drain the chestnuts and mash them in a large bowl – there is no need to make them particularly smooth.

2 Chop the onions and sauté them in the oil for a few minutes until tenderized. Add them to the bowl.

3 Add all the remaining ingredients and stir well. Transfer the mixture to a baking dish and bake in a moderate oven 350°F/180°C/Gas Mark 4 for about half an hour.

Chestnut Burgers

SERVE THIS EITHER WITH SALAD OR WITH GRAVY, A GREEN VEGETABLE SUCH AS BRUSSELS SPROUTS, AND POTATOES. A QUICK RECIPE.

$^1/_2$ pound/225g dried chestnuts which have been soaked in a Thermos flask (see page 104)

1 onion

1 tablespoon vegetable oil plus additional for frying burgers

1 teaspoon yeast extract

2 cups/4 oz/115g whole-wheat bread crumbs

$^1/_4$ cup/1 oz/30g soy flour

$^1/_2$ teaspoon dried sage

Sea salt as required

Freshly ground black pepper as required

$1^1/_3$ cups/10 fl oz/285ml hot water

1 Drain the chestnuts and mash them in a bowl.

2 Chop the onion finely. Sauté it in the oil until tender and beginning to brown. Add it to the mashed chestnuts.

3 Stir in the yeast extract, bread crumbs, soy flour, sage, and seasoning, then pour in the hot water. Mix with a spoon, then cool slightly and form into eight burgers.

4 Fry the burgers until browned on both sides.

Pasta

Pasta is without doubt one of the greatest culinary inventions ever. It is so easy to prepare and it can be used in so many ways. The only thing a vegan has to avoid is "pasta all uovo" (with eggs); fortunately most pasta is eggless.

Creole Noodles

OKRA ADDS AN EXOTIC TOUCH TO THIS EASY, SELF-CONTAINED DISH.

3/4 pound/340g whole-wheat noodles

2 onions

1/4 cup/2 oz/55g vegan margarine

2 green bell peppers

2 pounds/900g tomatoes

1/2 pound/225g green beans

4 oz/115g fresh okra

Sea salt as required

1 Cook the noodles for 10 minutes in boiling salted water, then leave them to drain.

2 Chop the onions and sauté them in the margarine until they begin to soften.

3 Peel and chop the tomatoes and chop the bell pepper and green beans. Trim the okra, cut them into small pieces and cover with boiling water for 1 minute, then drain.

4 Add all of the vegetables to the onions, cover and simmer for 20 minutes.

5 Add the noodles and cook until they are tender, adding water if necessary. Season to taste and serve.

Spaghetti with Tahini Sauce

IN THIS RECIPE, TAHINI, WHICH IS HIGH IN PROTEIN AND CALCIUM, FORMS THE BASIS OF A RICH, SATISFYING SPAGHETTI SAUCE. A QUICK RECIPE.

1/2 pound/225g whole-wheat spaghetti

2 onions

3 tablespoons vegetable oil

4 tablespoons tahini

4 tablespoons tomato paste

1 1/2–2 cups/10–15 fl oz/285–425ml water

2 teaspoons yeast extract

Freshly ground black pepper as required

1 Cook the spaghetti.

2 Meanwhile, chop the onions and fry them in the oil in a saucepan for a few minutes until lightly browned.

3 Add the tahini and tomato paste and then the water (start with the smaller quantity and if the sauce is too thick, add the rest). Bring to a boil, stirring constantly until thickened. Stir in the yeast extract and add pepper to taste. Simmer, uncovered, for a few minutes.

4 When the spaghetti is tender, drain it and pour the sauce over it.

Pasta with Mixed Vegetables

THIS HIGHLY NUTRITIOUS DISH REQUIRES NO ACCOMPANIMENTS.

4 tablespoons extra virgin olive oil

6–8 tablespoons minced parsley

6 scallions

2 cloves garlic

1 onion

1 tablespoon basil

$^1/_2$ small head cabbage

$^1/_2$ pound/225g zucchini

$^1/_2$ pound/225g tomatoes

2 green bell peppers

$1^1/_3$ cups/10 fl oz/285ml water

$^1/_2$ vegetable bouillon cube

2 teaspoons cider vinegar or wine
    vinegar

Sea salt as required

Freshly ground black pepper
    as required

12–14 oz/340–395g whole-wheat
    noodles or spaghetti

2 tablespoons/30g/1 oz vegan
    margarine

4 tablespoons soy bakon bits

1 Chop the scallions, garlic, and onion finely. Sauté them in the oil for 3 minutes.

2 Shred the cabbage, dice the zucchini and bell peppers, and peel and slice the tomatoes. Add these ingredients to the saucepan, together with the water, half bouillon cube, vinegar, basil, and seasoning.

3 Simmer, uncovered, for 10 minutes.

4 Cook the pasta until just tender, then drain and toss with the margarine.

5 Add the vegetable mixture, mix well, and sprinkle with the soy bakon bits.

Baked Noodles and Eggplant

THIS VARIATION ON A TRADITIONAL MIDDLE-EASTERN DISH CAN BE SERVED ON ITS OWN OR WITH SALAD. SUITABLE FOR A DINNER PARTY.

1½ pounds/680g eggplant

Sea salt as required

14 oz/395g whole-wheat noodles

1 large onion

1 clove garlic

3 tablespoons vegetable oil (or more if required)

2 large tomatoes

2 tablespoons tomato paste

½ teaspoon ground cinnamon

¼ teaspoon grated nutmeg

¼ teaspoon cayenne pepper

1 Cut the eggplant into slices.

2 Cook the noodles in boiling salted water until just tender. Drain and keep warm.

3 Chop the onion and garlic and sauté them in the oil until golden.

4 Add the eggplant slices and fry until lightly browned on both sides, using a little more oil if necessary.

5 Peel and chop the tomatoes and add them to the eggplant mixture along with the tomato paste. Season with the spices and add just a little water, simmering gently until the eggplant is tender and you have a thick sauce.

6 Place alternate layers of pasta and sauce in an oiled casserole dish.

7 Bake in a moderate oven at 350°F/180°C/Gas Mark 4 for about half an hour. Alternatively, cover with wax paper and microwave for 7–8 minutes.

Pasta, Broccoli, and Mushroom Casserole with Cashew & Pimento Cheese

CASHEW & PIMENTO CHEESE

1 cup/¼ pound/115g cashew pieces

1 small can (7 oz/200g) pimentos

Juice of ¼ lemon

2 tablespoons vegetable oil

2 tablespoons nutritional yeast

1 tablespoon water

1 tablespoon soy sauce

Sea salt as required

Freshly ground black pepper
   as required

3 cups/¾ pound/340g whole-wheat
   pasta shells (or other shape)

¾ pound/340g broccoli

2 tablespoons vegetable oil

2 onions

2 cloves garlic

6 cups/¾ pound/340g mushrooms

1 Put the cashews into a liquidizer or food processor and grind them. Add all the remaining "cheese" ingredients and blend thoroughly.

2 Cook the pasta until just tender and drain.

3 Cook the broccoli until just tender and drain.

4 Heat the oil in a skillet. Chop the onions and sauté them in the oil. Chop the garlic finely and add to the pan. Continue to cook for a few minutes while cleaning and chopping the mushrooms. Add the mushrooms and sauté for a few minutes longer.

5 In a large saucepan or bowl mix the pasta, broccoli, and contents of the skillet with the "cheese" mixture. Transfer to an oiled casserole dish and bake at 350°F/180°C/Gas Mark 4 for about half an hour. Alternatively, cover with wax paper and microwave for 7–8 minutes.

Pasta in Forno

PASTA DISHES COOKED IN THE OVEN ("IN FORNO") ARE THE ONLY KIND WHICH THE ITALIANS CONSIDER TO BE TRUE MAIN DISHES.

3–3½ cups/12–14 oz/340–395g whole-wheat shells (or other shape)

2 onions

¼ cup/2 oz/55g vegan margarine

2 tablespoons olive oil

2 cloves garlic

1 green bell pepper

1 pound/455g eggplant

1½ pounds/680g tomatoes

1 teaspoon dried oregano

1 teaspoon dried basil

Sea salt as required

Freshly ground black pepper
   as required

4 tablespoons water

¼ cup/1 oz/30g nutritional yeast or 2
   tablespoons vegan Parmesan

1 Cook the pasta until just tender.

2 Meanwhile, chop the onion and fry it in half the margarine and the oil for 2–3 minutes. Chop the garlic finely, add it to the pan and fry for 2–3 minutes.

3 Chop the bell pepper finely. Dice the eggplant. Skin and chop the tomatoes. Add these ingredients to the pan, together with the herbs, seasoning, and water. Bring to a boil, then lower the heat, cover and simmer for a few minutes until the vegetables are just tender.

4 Mix the pasta with the vegetables and transfer to a large oiled casserole dish. Sprinkle with yeast or vegan Parmesan and dot with the remainder of the margarine. Bake at 350°F/180°C/Gas Mark 4 for about half an hour. Alternatively, cover with wax paper and microwave for 7–8 minutes.

Tangy Noodle Casserole

THE IDEA FOR THIS RECIPE IS BASED ON AN EASTERN EUROPEAN DISH OF NOODLES WITH COTTAGE CHEESE. SERVE IT WITH SEASONAL VEGETABLES.

10 oz/285g whole-wheat noodles

2 cups/1 pound/455g tofu

1½ tablespoons lemon juice

1 tablespoon vegetable oil

2 tablespoons miso

3 scallions

1 tablespoon vegan margarine

1 Cook the noodles until tender in lightly salted water and drain.

2 Put half the tofu in a liquidizer along with the lemon juice, oil and miso, and blend thoroughly.

3 Put the other half of the tofu into a clean dish towel and squeeze as much of the moisture out as possible.

4 Chop the scallions finely.

5 In a large bowl combine the noodles, tofu/miso mixture, squeezed tofu, and chopped scallions. Mix well, then turn into an oiled casserole dish.

6 Dot the top of the mixture with small pieces of margarine, cover and bake at 350°F/180°C/Gas Mark 4 for 20 minutes, then uncover and bake for another 10 minutes.

Macaroni, Mushroom, and Tofu Casserole

SERVE WITH EITHER COOKED SEASONAL VEGETABLES OR SALAD.

1 cup/$^1/_2$ pound/225g tofu

Vegetable oil for deep-frying as
   required

2 cups/$^1/_2$ pound/225g whole-wheat
   macaroni

4 cups/$^1/_2$ pound/225g mushrooms

4 tablespoons vegan margarine

2 teaspoons lemon juice

3 tablespoons whole-wheat flour

1$^1/_3$ cups/10 fl oz/285ml soy milk

2 teaspoons miso

Freshly ground black pepper as
   required

Nutritional yeast as required or 2
   tablespoons vegan Parmesan

1 Cube the tofu and deep-fry until golden. Set aside.

2 Cook the macaroni until tender and set aside.

3 Slice the mushrooms and sauté them in 1 tablespoon
   margarine until just tender. Sprinkle the lemon juice over
   them and set aside.

4 Melt the remainder of the margarine in a saucepan and stir
   in the flour. Slowly add the milk, stirring constantly to avoid
   lumps. Remove from the heat and stir in the miso and
   pepper.

5 Add the cooked macaroni, fried tofu cubes, and sautéed
   mushrooms to the sauce and mix well. Turn into an oiled
   casserole dish, sprinkle with yeast or vegan Parmesan, and
   place in the oven at 350°F/180°C/Gas Mark 4 for about 15
   minutes. Alternatively, cover with wax paper and microwave
   for about 6 minutes.

Spaghetti with Tempeh Sauce

THIS IS SIMILAR TO A TRADITIONAL "BOLOGNESE" SAUCE, MADE WITH TEMPEH INSTEAD OF MEAT.

2 onions

1–2 cloves garlic

2 tablespoons extra virgin olive oil

2 sticks celery

2 cups/4 oz/115g mushrooms

1 can (14–16 oz/400g) tomatoes

4 tablespoons tomato paste

²/₃ cup/5 fl oz/140ml water

3 teaspoons dried basil

2 teaspoons dried marjoram

Sea salt as required

Freshly ground black pepper
    as required

1 cup/¹/₂ pound/225g tempeh

12 oz/340g whole-wheat spaghetti

1 Chop the onions and garlic finely. Sauté in the oil for 2–3 minutes.

2 Chop the celery and mushrooms and add them to the saucepan. Stir well and cook for 2–3 minutes.

3 Add the tomatoes (mashing them with a spoon while doing so), tomato paste, water, herbs, and seasoning. Crumble the tempeh into the saucepan. Stir well. Bring to the boil, then lower the heat and simmer for about 20 minutes, stirring occasionally while the spaghetti is cooking.

4 Drain the spaghetti thoroughly. Mix the sauce through the spaghetti and serve.

Sea Vegetables

Sea vegetables are greatly underused in much of our cooking. Very low in calories, totally fat free, loaded with vitamins and minerals, they add a whole new range of tastes to meals, a real "tang of the sea". Of course the texture of sea vegetables is quite different from that of sea fish and other non-vegan sea foods, but combine sea vegetables with the meaty textures of tofu or tempeh and you'll get both the taste and texture of classic sea food dishes.

Most sea vegetables are purchased dried, and only a small amount will be needed at a time as they will swell to twice their dry weight when refreshed.

Perhaps the main reason sea vegetables are not used more often is that many people do not know quite what to do with them. This selection of recipes should help point you in the right direction – and will open up a new range of ingredients to you.

SEA VEGETABLE GUIDE

KOMBU *A type of kelp, a bit tough and chewy but full of flavor. Soak for at least 10 minutes before using.*

WAKAME *A softer, greenish leaf with a hard stem. You should discard the stem, rinse the leaves well and soak for about 10 minutes before using.*

HIJIKI *Sometimes spelled* hiziki. *This is probably the most accessible sea vegetable – and tends to be well liked even by those determined not to enjoy sea vegetables! It comes in thin strips and should be soaked for about 20 minutes before cooking. It is good served cold in salads.*

ARAME *Looks very like hijiki but it has been shredded after picking as in its natural form it has a wide leaf. It has a sweeter taste than hijiki.*

DULSE *This sea vegetable can be found growing naturally around the British coast. It has a strong flavor and goes well in stews. It shouldn't require pre-soaking but do check the instructions on the packet you buy.*

NORI *This is quite different from any of the other sea vegetables and is the one which more people are likely to have already tried as it is often used as the outer layer of Japanese rice sushi. Nori comes in sheets which should be toasted over a flame for a couple of minutes, until the color changes. Your nori is then ready to eat.*

Arame and Peanut Stir-fry

THIS CLASSIC ORIENTAL STIR-FRY IS BEST SERVED OVER BROWN RICE. THE BEST PEANUTS TO USE ARE
UNSALTED DRY-ROASTED PEANUTS AVAILABLE AT SOME HEALTH-FOOD STORES AND SUPERMARKETS.
ALTERNATIVELY, USE WHOLE PEANUTS WHICH YOU HAVE SHELLED. A QUICK RECIPE.

1 oz/30g dried arame

1 large green bell pepper

2 large carrots

4 cups/$^1/_2$ pound/225g mushrooms

10–12 scallions

1 or 2 cloves garlic

2 tablespoons vegetable oil

2 teaspoons finely grated fresh ginger

2 tablespoons soy sauce

$^3/_4$ cup/4 oz/115g roasted peanuts

Brown rice as required

1 Soak the arame in cold water for about 10 minutes.

2 Slice the bell pepper, carrots, and mushrooms thinly. Chop
the scallions and garlic finely.

3 Heat the oil in a wok or skillet. Add all the vegetables and
stir-fry for 3–4 minutes.

4 Drain the arame and add it to the wok together with the soy
sauce and fresh ginger. Mix in well and stir-fry for another
2–3 minutes.

Arame and Tofu Pancakes

Crêpe batter (see page 288)

1 oz/30g arame

3 tablespoons vegan margarine

$^1/_3$ cup/$1^1/_2$ oz/40g whole-wheat flour

2 cups/15 fl oz/425ml soy milk

2 tablespoons soy sauce

Sea salt as required

Freshly ground black pepper
   as required

3 tablespoons vegetarian
   Worcestershire sauce

1 cup/$^1/_2$ pound/225g tofu

$^2/_3$ cup/5 fl oz/140ml soy yogurt

5 tablespoons nutritional yeast

1 Cover the arame with cold water in a saucepan, bring to a boil, lower the heat and simmer for about 5 minutes. Drain and chop.

2 Heat the margarine in a saucepan and stir in the flour. Gradually add the milk, stirring constantly to avoid lumps. When it has thickened simmer for a minute or two, then season with the sauces, salt, and pepper. Crumble in the tofu and stir in the chopped arame. Mix well.

3 Fry the crêpes (there should be 4–5 per person) and fill each with the arame/tofu mixture before folding them over or rolling them up.

4 In a small bowl mix together the soy yogurt and yeast. When all the crêpes have been filled, spoon the yogurt mixture over the top. Place all the crêpes under a fairly hot broiler until the yogurt is well heated and serve immediately.

Arame Pasta Pie

THIS RECIPE IS SIMPLE AND YET VERY EFFECTIVE.

2–3 cups/$^1/_2$–$^3/_4$ pound/225–340g small
    whole-wheat pasta shapes
1 oz/30g arame
3 cups/25 fl oz/750ml soy milk
2 onions
2 tablespoons vegetable oil
$^1/_4$ cup/1 oz/30g whole-wheat flour
2 tablespoons soy sauce
Sea salt as required
Freshly ground black pepper
    as required
Whole-wheat bread crumbs or
    nutritional yeast as required
2 tablespoons/1 oz/30g vegan
    margarine

1 Cook the pasta until just tender and set aside.
2 Put the arame in a saucepan, cover with cold water, bring to
a boil, then lower the heat and simmer for about 5 minutes.
Drain the arame, cool it slightly (by pouring cold water over
it if desired) and chop it.
3 Heat the milk in a saucepan. When it is boiling, lower the
heat and add the arame. Let it simmer, uncovered, for a few
minutes.
4 Chop the onions finely. Heat the oil in a large saucepan and
sauté them for a few minutes until just beginning to turn
brown. Stir in the flour, then add the milk and arame,
stirring constantly to avoid lumps. When it is thick and
smooth stir in the soy sauce and seasoning.
5 Turn the mixture into a casserole dish and sprinkle bread
crumbs or yeast on top. Add shavings of the margarine.
Bake at 375°F/190°C/Gas Mark 5 for about 20 minutes.
Alternatively, cover with wax paper and microwave for
5–6 minutes.

Millet and Arame Bake

THIS DISH COMBINES A RARELY USED GRAIN WITH A MILD-FLAVORED SEA VEGETABLE AND LOTS OF OTHER TASTY INGREDIENTS.

1⅓ cups/½ pound/225g millet

3 cups/25 fl oz/750ml water

Pinch of sea salt

1 oz/30g arame

2 onions

2 tablespoons vegetable oil

2 green bell peppers

4 cups/½ pound/225g mushrooms

2 tablespoons whole-wheat flour

¾ cup/6 fl oz/180ml soy milk

1 teaspoon ground ginger

2 tablespoons soy sauce

½ cup/2 oz/55g almonds

Sea salt as required

Freshly ground black pepper
  as required

1 Dry roast the millet in a large heavy saucepan for a few minutes until it smells aromatic. Add the water and salt. Bring to a boil, lower the heat, cover the pan, and simmer until the water is absorbed – about 20 minutes.

2 Cover the arame with cold water in a saucepan, bring to a boil and simmer for a few minutes. Drain and set aside. Chop the almonds in half and set aside.

3 Chop the onions and sauté them in the oil in a large saucepan. Chop the bell peppers and mushrooms and add them to the pan. Cook for a few more minutes, then sprinkle in the flour. Stir well, then gradually add the milk, stirring constantly until thickened. Add the ginger and soy sauce.

4 Remove the saucepan from the heat. Stir in the cooked millet, arame, and almonds. Add seasoning to taste.

5 Turn the whole mixture into a large casserole dish and bake at 350°F/180°C/Gas Mark 4 for about half an hour. Alternatively, cover with wax paper and microwave for 6–7 minutes.

Dulse and Vegetable Stew

THE DULSE WILL ALMOST DISSOLVE IN THE OAT AND VEGETABLE MIXTURE, TO GIVE A LOVELY FLAVOR TO THE STEW. SERVE IT WITH THICK SLICES OF WHOLE-WHEAT BREAD.

1 cup/4 oz/115g rolled oats

5 cups/40 fl oz/1120ml water

2–3 tablespoons vegetable oil

1 oz/30g dulse

4 sticks celery

$^1/_2$ pound/225g carrots

$^1/_2$ pound/225g potatoes

1 large or 2 small onions

4 cups/$^1/_2$ pound/225g mushrooms

2–3 tablespoons soy sauce

Sea salt as required

Freshly ground black pepper
  as required

1 Put the oats and water in a saucepan and bring to a boil. Lower the heat, cover the pan, and leave to simmer.

2 Chop the dulse and set aside.

3 Chop all the vegetables finely, and sauté them in the oil in a wok or skillet for 3–4 minutes. Add them to the saucepan, together with the dulse, and simmer for about half an hour, stirring occasionally.

4 Add the soy sauce and seasoning to taste, before serving.

Hijiki and Vegetables

THIS FAR-EASTERN DISH SHOULD BE SERVED OVER BROWN RICE.

1 oz/30g hijiki

4 cups/½ pound/225g mushrooms

3 scallions

2 tablespoons vegetable oil

½ pound/225g green beans

2 small white turnips

1 tablespoon soy sauce

4 cups/½ pound/225g mung bean
   sprouts

1 tablespoon arrowroot

¾ cup/7 fl oz/200ml water

Brown rice as required

1 tablespoon soy sauce

1 Rinse the hijiki well by covering with water and draining two or three times. Now soak it in enough water to cover for about 20 minutes.

2 Slice the mushrooms and scallions and stir-fry in the oil in a wok or skillet for about 3 minutes. Add the drained hijiki and stir well.

3 Peel and dice the turnips; slice the green beans. Add about three-quarters of the water to the pan, together with the turnip and beans. Bring to a boil, cover and leave to steam for a few minutes.

4 Remove the lid, add the bean sprouts and soy sauce and stir well. Mix the arrowroot with the remainder of the water and add to the mixture. Stir well until it thickens.

Tempeh Fillets with Hijiki

SERVE THIS SIMPLE DISH WITH LIGHTLY COOKED SEASONAL VEGETABLES.

1 oz/30g hijiki

1¹⁄₃ cups/10 fl oz/285ml warm water

6 teaspoons miso

1 pound/455g tempeh

1 Rinse the hijiki under cold water. Cover it with warm water and leave to soak for about 30 minutes.

2 Combine the water and miso in a food processor and blend well. Pour into a large saucepan. Slice each of the ¹⁄₂ pound tempeh blocks in half. Put them into the saucepan. Drain the hijiki and add to the saucepan.

3 Simmer, covered, over a very low heat for about 10 minutes. Turn the tempeh fillets over. Add a little additional water if it seems necessary. Cook for another 10 minutes. Serve each tempeh fillet topped with hijiki.

Hijiki Sauce for Pasta

AS NON-VEGAN "SEAFOODS" ARE USED IN PASTA SAUCES, THERE'S NO REASON WHY A VEGAN SEAFOOD SHOULD NOT FEATURE IN A PASTA SAUCE TOO.

1¹⁄₂ oz/45g hijiki

1 onion

1–2 cloves garlic

1 green bell pepper

2 tablespoons extra virgin olive oil

2 cans (14–16 oz/400g each) tomatoes

2 teaspoons dried oregano

Black pepper as required

1 Rinse the hijiki under cold water. Cover it with warm water and leave to soak for about 30 minutes.

2 Chop the onion, garlic, and bell pepper finely. Sauté them in the oil for 3–4 minutes.

3 Purée the tomatoes in a liquidizer. Add to the saucepan, along with the oregano. Bring to a boil then simmer, uncovered, for about 5 minutes. Add the soaked and drained hijiki and cook for 15–20 minutes, stirring occasionally.

4 Grind in the pepper and serve over pasta.

Hijiki, Smoked Tofu, and Sunflower Pie

THIS IS A VERY SIMPLE DISH, WITH FEW INGREDIENTS, AS THE SMOKED TOFU AND HIJIKI HAVE ENOUGH FLAVOR OF THEIR OWN. THE SUNFLOWER SEEDS ADD AN INTERESTING TEXTURE CONTRAST. SERVE WITH ZUCCHINI OR ANY PREFERRED VEGETABLE.

1 oz/30g hijiki
2–3 cups/1–1½ pounds/455–680g
    smoked tofu
½ cup/2 oz/55g sunflower seeds
3–4 cups/1½–2 pounds/680–900g
    mashed potato

1 Soak the hijiki in cold water for about 20 minutes, then cook it for a few minutes until tender. Drain and cool it (by running cold water over it if desired to save time).
2 Put the smoked tofu into a bowl and mash it well.
3 Chop the hijiki and add it to the tofu together with the sunflower seeds. Mix well and transfer to an ovenproof dish.
4 Spoon the mashed potato on top. Bake at 375°F/190°C/Gas Mark 5 for 20–30 minutes.

Hijiki and Cashew Ragout

THIS TAKES NO TIME AT ALL. SERVE WITH BAKED OR BOILED POTATOES.

2 oz/55g hijiki

2 cups/½ pound/225g whole cashews

4 onions

3 tablespoons vegetable oil

4 tomatoes

3 tablespoons whole-wheat flour

3 tablespoons soy sauce or to taste

Sea salt as required

Freshly ground black pepper
   as required

1 Clean, soak, and cook the hijiki until tender. Drain well.

2 Place the cashews under a hot broiler and turn them frequently to brown evenly.

3 Chop the onions and sauté them in the oil in a saucepan until just transparent.

4 Chop the tomatoes and add them to the pan. Cook until tender.

5 Sprinkle the flour in and stir well. Slowly stir in enough water to make a thick sauce.

6 Add the cooked hijiki to the pan, then add the soy sauce and seasoning to taste. Stir in the cashews at the last minute.

Lentil and Kombu Stew

KOMBU HELPS TO TENDERIZE LENTILS AND SPEEDS UP THE COOKING PROCESS. SERVE THE STEW WITH WEDGES OF WHOLE-WHEAT BREAD.

1 cup/6 oz/170g brown lentils
1/2 oz/15g kombu
1 bay leaf
3 3/4 cups/30 fl oz/850ml water
1 onion
1 large or 2 small leeks
2 tablespoons vegetable oil
1 large or 2 small carrots
Sea salt as required
Freshly ground black pepper
    as required

1 Place the lentils and kombu in a large saucepan and cover with plenty of cold water. Leave to soak for a few hours.
2 Drain the lentils and kombu. Remove the kombu and chop it into bite-sized pieces. Return the lentils and kombu to the saucepan; add the bay leaf and 3 3/4 cups/30 fl oz/850ml water, cover and bring to a boil. Lower the heat and simmer for 15–20 minutes.
3 Chop the onion and leek. Heat the oil in a skillet and sauté them for 2–3 minutes. Dice the carrot and add to the pan; stir-fry for a minute or two.
4 Add the vegetables to the lentil/kombu mixture and stir well. Add the seasoning. Continue cooking for 10–20 minutes before serving.

Wakame and Vegetable Stew

SERVE THIS APPEALING STEW WITH WHOLE-WHEAT BREAD.

1 oz/30g wakame
2 onions
2 1/2 cups/20 fl oz/570ml water
3/4 pound/340g carrots
1 1/2 pound/680g potatoes
3/4 pound/340g Brussels sprouts
4 tablespoons soy sauce

1 Soak the wakame for about 10 minutes, drain, and chop.
2 Chop the onions coarsely. Put them in a large saucepan with the wakame and cover with the water. Bring to a boil, then lower the heat and simmer, uncovered, for about 5 minutes.
3 Chop the carrots and potatoes into small pieces. Halve or quarter the Brussels sprouts. Add them to the saucepan, together with the soy sauce, and simmer for 15–20 minutes until the potato is tender.

Wakame and Potato Casserole with a Tofu Topping

TOFU COMBINES WELL WITH A SEA VEGETABLE LIKE WAKAME.

1¹/₂ pound/680g potatoes

1 oz/30g wakame

2¹/₂ cups/1¹/₄ pound/565g tofu

6–8 tablespoons soy milk

1 tablespoon tahini

2 teaspoons lemon juice

1 tablespoon soy sauce

Sea salt as required

Freshly ground black pepper
   as required

4 scallions

1 Cook the potatoes until tender (or use leftover cooked potatoes).

2 Soak the wakame in cold water for about 10 minutes. Drain and chop it, discarding the central frond.

3 Put the tofu, soy milk, tahini, lemon juice, and 1 tablespoon soy sauce (plus additional seasoning if desired) into a liquidizer or food processor and blend thoroughly.

4 Slice the cooked potatoes. Chop the scallions finely. In the bottom of a casserole put a layer of potatoes, then a layer of chopped wakame, a sprinkling of minced scallion, and a little soy sauce. Repeat the layers until all the ingredients have been used.

5 Spoon the tofu mixture over the top, and bake at 375°F/190°C/Gas Mark 5 for about 40 minutes.

Vegetable Stir-fry with Nori

NORI IS CERTAINLY THE EASIEST SEA VEGETABLE TO USE. SERVE THIS OVER BROWN RICE.

10–12 dried mushrooms

2 onions

2 tablespoons vegetable oil

2 cloves garlic

2 teaspoons finely grated fresh ginger

$^1/_2$ pound/225g carrots

$^1/_2$ pound/225g cabbage

1 large green bell pepper

1 teaspoon cider vinegar or wine
   vinegar

2 tablespoons soy sauce

2 sheets nori

1 Soak the mushrooms in warm water for about half an hour.

2 Chop the onions. Heat the oil in a wok or skillet and sauté the onions for a minute or two.

3 Mince the garlic. Add to the wok with the ginger. Continue stir-frying for a minute or two longer.

4 Chop the carrots, cabbage, and bell pepper finely. Add to the wok and stir-fry for 2–3 minutes.

5 Drain the mushrooms, reserving some of the liquid. Chop them and add to the pan, along with 4 tablespoons of the soaking liquid, the vinegar, and the soy sauce. Cook for a few minutes longer.

6 Toast the nori (see instructions on page 134). Crumble it into the vegetables and serve at once.

Creamy Rice and Nori Savory

IF YOU HAVE LEFTOVER RICE, THIS IS A VERY SPEEDY DISH. SERVE IT WITH SEASONAL VEGETABLES.

1½–2 cups/10–12 oz/285–340g brown rice

3 tablespoons vegan margarine

3 tablespoons whole-wheat flour

3 cups/25 fl oz/750ml soy milk

2 tablespoons soy sauce

1 teaspoon mustard

2–3 sheets nori

1½ cups/3 oz/85g whole-wheat bread crumbs

1 Cook the rice (or use rice which has already been cooked).

2 Melt the margarine in a saucepan. Stir in the flour and then the milk. Stir constantly until it has thickened to avoid lumps. Season with soy sauce and mustard. Remove from the heat.

3 Stir the rice into the sauce. Toast the nori, crumble it, and stir it into the mixture. Spoon the mixture into a baking dish and cover with the bread crumbs.

4 Bake at 400°F/200°C/Gas Mark 6 for 15–20 minutes. Alternatively, cover with wax paper and microwave for 5–6 minutes, browning it under broiler if desired.

Kedgeree

NORI AND SMOKED TOFU MAKE A LOVELY COMBINATION. A QUICK RECIPE.

1½–2 cups/10–12 oz/285–340g brown rice

2 sheets nori

½ cup/4 oz/115g vegan margarine

1½–2 cups/¾–1 pound/340–455g smoked tofu

Sea salt as required

Cayenne pepper as required

4 tablespoons minced parsley

1 Cook the rice until tender (or use leftover cooked rice).

2 Toast the nori and set aside.

3 Melt the margarine in a large saucepan. Dice the smoked tofu and add it to the pan; sauté until lightly browned. Add the cooked rice to the pan and continue to cook, stirring well. Shred the toasted nori into the mixture. Season with salt and cayenne. Sprinkle with the parsley and serve.

Tofu Nori Savory

2 sheets nori

2¹/₂–3 cups/1¹/₄–1¹/₂ pound/565–680g
tofu

¹/₂ cup/2 oz/55g vegan margarine (plus
extra as required)

3 tablespoons/1¹/₂ oz/45g whole-wheat
flour

2¹/₂ cups/20 fl oz/570ml soy milk

Sea salt as required

Freshly ground black pepper as required

2 teaspoons curry powder

4 tablespoons whole-wheat
bread crumbs

1 Toast the nori. Slice the tofu and place half the slices in an
oiled baking dish. Tear half the nori into pieces and place
on top of the tofu; repeat with the second half of the tofu
and nori.

2 Melt ¹/₂ cup/2 oz/55g margarine in a saucepan and stir in the
flour. Slowly add the milk, stirring constantly to avoid
lumps, until it comes to a boil. Season well and stir in the
curry powder; cook for a minute or two longer.

3 Pour the sauce over the tofu/nori layers. Sprinkle with the
bread crumbs and top with shavings of margarine. Bake at
350°F/180°C/Gas Mark 4 for about half an hour.

Nori and Potato Casserole

THE IDEA FOR THIS DISH CAME FROM A SCANDINAVIAN FISH RECIPE. SERVE IT WITH A SEASONAL GREEN VEGETABLE.

2 pounds/900g potatoes

1 small onion

3 sheets nori

2 tablespoons/1 oz/30g vegan
   margarine

2$\frac{1}{2}$ cups/20 fl oz/570ml soy milk

1 cup/$\frac{1}{2}$ pound/225g tofu

2 tablespoons soy sauce

Sea salt as required

Freshly ground black pepper
   as required

$\frac{1}{2}$ cup/1 oz/30g bread crumbs

1 Cook the potatoes (or use leftover potatoes). Slice them thickly (peeled if preferred). Chop the onion finely. Toast the nori and tear it into strips.

2 Layer the potato slices, onion, and nori in an oiled baking dish, ending with a layer of potato. Put shavings of the margarine on top.

3 Blend the milk, tofu, and soy sauce in a liquidizer. Season to taste.

4 Pour the blended mixture over the potato casserole. Top with bread crumbs. Bake at 350°F/180°C/Gas Mark 4 for 30–40 minutes (the longer time if the potatoes are leftovers from the refrigerator).

Tofu Specialty Dishes

Used in the Far East for centuries, it is only in the past two or three decades that tofu (also known as "soy bean curd") has appeared in the West. It's well known that soy is a valuable source of plant proteins – but uncooked soy beans are not at all easy to digest. Tofu enables us to enjoy the protein and goodness of soy in an easily digestible form.

By extracting the soy "milk" and curdling it, we make tofu. There are basically three types of tofu: silken tofu which is very soft, medium tofu which is firmer (you could lift it but would need to be careful as a piece could break off), and firm tofu which can be held up as a block without breaking. Health-food or grocery stores that stock tofu will normally offer all three types.

TOFU TYPES

SILKEN TOFU *Is a pure, high-quality product with a distinctive flavor. It is a Japanese product and is made in a different way from other types of tofu – it maintains its soft texture because the curds and whey are not separated. It is particularly useful in desserts, dressings, and sauces, and keeps without refrigeration for months.*

MEDIUM TOFU *Is readily available and, if you ever make your own tofu at home, you are likely to produce this type. The medium tofu found in Chinese supermarkets has a stronger flavor than the similar Japanese "house" tofu, so although it's fine for traditional Chinese recipes, you may sometimes prefer to use the slightly sweeter Japanese version. If you're deep frying though, stick with the Chinese product as it's by far the more suitable for this purpose.*

FIRM TOFU *This is the kind you can buy vacuum packed in slices and chunks. It can be puréed if your recipe calls for a softer tofu.*

SMOKED TOFU *The process of smoking gives an entirely new texture and a delicious taste. Smoked tofu is excellent "raw" straight from the packet and makes a useful meat-free alternative sliced in sandwiches or diced into salads. It also works well broiled or crispy fried.*

MARINATED TOFU *One of the most popular ways of preparing tofu is to marinate it in a mixture of soy sauce and ginger. Tofu readily absorbs flavors so marinating is the perfect way to prepare tofu for a stir-fry.*

FERMENTED TOFU *This can be found in jars and cans at Chinese supermarkets. Said to be a little like French Camembert, it is much more salty than cheese and is not really suitable to be eaten on its own. Used sparingly to highlight other flavors, its distinctive flavor adds a twist to recipes.*

FROZEN TOFU *Ordinary tofu can be frozen – and when thawed you'll notice it has a much "meatier" texture than before. It is a good idea to slice the tofu before freezing it. The best way to thaw your frozen tofu slices is to pour over boiling water and leave for about 10 minutes. Then drain the slices and squeeze any excess water out of them.*

Mushroom Stroganoff

IN THIS RECIPE THE TOFU IS LIQUIFIED INTO A RICH CREAM. SERVE IT OVER COOKED NOODLES. A QUICK RECIPE.

1 pound/455g mushrooms
4 tablespoons vegetable oil
1 clove garlic
1 onion
$^1/_2$ cup/2 oz/55g whole-wheat flour
2 cups/15 fl oz/425ml vegetable
   bouillon
1$^1/_2$ cups/$^3/_4$ pound/340g tofu
Sea salt as required
Freshly ground black pepper
   as required
Mustard powder as required

1 Slice the mushrooms and sauté them in the oil until tender.
2 Chop the garlic and onion finely and add them to the saucepan. Sauté for another 5 minutes.
3 Add the flour, stirring well. Slowly add the vegetable bouillon, stirring constantly to avoid lumps. Cook for a minute or two.
4 Put the tofu in the liquidizer and add enough water to make about 2$^1/_2$ cups/20 fl oz/570ml of tofu cream. Blend thoroughly.
5 Add the tofu cream to the mushroom mixture, stirring well. Season and cook until well heated.

Tofu and Onions

THIS IS A VERY SIMPLE DISH WHICH IS BEST SERVED OVER BROWN RICE. A QUICK RECIPE.

3 onions
3 tablespoons vegetable oil
2 cups/1 pound/455g tofu
2 teaspoons cornstarch
$^2/_3$ cup/5 fl oz/140ml water
2 teaspoons soy sauce

1 Slice the onions thinly and sauté them in oil until tender.
2 Cut the tofu into small cubes and add them to the onions. Stir well.
3 Combine the cornstarch with the water and soy sauce. Pour the mixture over the tofu and onions. Bring to a boil, stirring constantly until thickened.
4 Simmer for 2–3 minutes before serving.

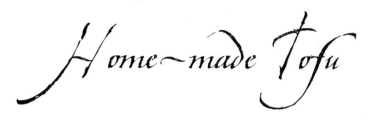

Home-made Tofu

1 cup/¹/₂ pound/225g soy beans
Boiling water as required
Cold water as required
1 heaped teaspoon nigari, lemon juice,
   or Epsom salts

1 The night before, cover the beans with boiling water and leave them to soak. In the morning drain and rinse. Place a cup of the soaked beans in the liquidizer, add a cup of cold water and blend. Then add about 2 cups of boiling water to the liquidizer and blend again. *Note*: if your liquidizer is not large enough then a smaller quantity can be done each time as long as the proportions are kept more or less the same – it is *not* necessary to measure with any great precision when making tofu.

2 Place a large piece of cheesecloth over a saucepan and carefully pour the contents of the liquidizer into it. Pull up the sides to make it into a sack so that the soy milk runs through, and squeeze gently to get all of the liquid into the saucepan. (The pulp left in the muslin is called "okara" and can be used in savory dishes; it is high in protein but, unlike tofu, is not very easy to digest.)

3 Once all of the beans have been used up put the saucepan of soy milk on to a medium to high heat and bring to a boil, stirring the bottom from time to time. Keep a careful eye on it because it can boil over very suddenly and dramatically. As soon as it starts to boil turn the heat right down very low so it is still simmering but no longer threatening to erupt. Leave to simmer for about three minutes.

4 Meanwhile, put the heaped teaspoon of nigari, lemon juice, or Epsom salts into a cup. Fill it half full of boiling water and stir well. Remove the soy milk from the heat, then gently stir in the dissolved coagulant, trying to make certain it has been stirred through all of the liquid. Leave for about three minutes, by which time curds should have formed.

5 Place a piece of muslin or a muslin-lined box in a colander, then gradually pour the contents of the saucepan into it, so that the whey runs through and the curds settle in the box. Then put the colander over the empty saucepan to continue to drain, and place something heavy (about 2 pounds/900g)

on top. Leave for an hour or so before unmolding. Half a pound (225g) of soy beans will make about 1½ cups/¾ pound/340g of tofu (though it can vary by ¼ cup/2 oz/55g either way).

6 If the tofu is not to be used immediately it should be stored in the refrigerator in an airtight container of water, where it will keep for about a week. (Most instructions tell you to change the water every day, but if the container is left undisturbed then this really is not necessary.)

Tofu Kebabs

THIS IS A DIFFERENT WAY OF COOKING TOFU. SERVE IT IN PITTA BREAD OR OVER RICE.

2 cups/1 pound/455g firm tofu
2 tablespoons extra virgin olive oil
2 tablespoons cider vinegar or wine vinegar
3 tablespoons mustard
2 teaspoons dried rosemary
1 teaspoon dried sage
2 teaspoons sea salt
1 teaspoon freshly ground black pepper
2 cups/4 oz/115g mushrooms
1 green bell pepper

1 Drain the tofu and wrap it in a clean dish towel for a few minutes to get rid of excess moisture. Cut it into cubes.

2 In a large bowl combine the oil, vinegar, mustard, herbs, and seasonings. (*Note:* Dried rosemary can be rather coarse; with a mortar and pestle it is easy to grind it to a powder.)

3 Put the tofu cubes into the bowl and stir them well so that the mustard mixture adheres to them.

4 Cover the bowl and put it into the refrigerator. Leave it to marinate for 2–3 hours, turning the tofu cubes once or twice.

5 Clean the mushrooms and remove the stalks. Chop the bell pepper into chunks large enough to be threaded on to a skewer.

6 Thread the tofu cubes onto skewers, alternating with the bell pepper and mushrooms. Place them on a broiler pan under a hot broiler. Broil, turning the skewers from time to time, until they are nicely browned all over. Serve immediately.

Tofu Casserole

DEEP FRYING TOFU GIVES IT A LIGHT CHEWY TEXTURE WHICH, IN THIS RECIPE, FORMS A CONTRAST TO A
CREAMY WHITE SAUCE. SERVE THE CASSEROLE WITH SEASONAL VEGETABLES AND POTATOES.

2 cups/1 pound/455g tofu

Vegetable oil as required for
deep frying

2 small or 1 large onion

2 cloves garlic

3 tablespoons/1½ oz/45g vegan
margarine

¼ cup/1 oz/30g whole-wheat flour

1⅓ cups/10 fl oz/285ml soy milk

2 tablespoons miso

Freshly ground black pepper as
required

1 cup/2 oz/55g whole-wheat
bread crumbs

1 Cube the tofu and deep fry until golden. (This may be done
   in advance, and the cubes kept in the refrigerator until
   cooking time.)

2 Slice the onions thinly. Mince the garlic. Sauté in 2
   tablespoons/1 oz/30g of the margarine for 4–5 minutes,
   until softened and lightly browned.

3 Stir the flour into the onions. Gradually add the milk,
   stirring constantly to avoid lumps. Bring to a boil and, when
   thickened, remove from the heat. Immediately stir in the
   miso, and continue stirring well until smooth. Add pepper to
   taste, then stir in the tofu cubes.

4 Turn the mixture into an oiled baking dish, sprinkle with
   the bread crumbs, dot with the remaining margarine and
   bake in the oven at 350°F/180°C/Gas Mark 4 for about 20
   minutes. Alternatively, cover with wax paper and microwave
   for 5–6 minutes.

Warming Winter Stew

DEEP-FRIED TOFU ALSO WORKS WELL IN A STEW. THIS IS GOOD OVER BROWN RICE OR, ALTERNATIVELY, ON ITS OWN, ACCOMPANIED BY POTATOES OR BREAD.

2 cups/1 pound/455g tofu

2 tablespoons vegetable oil plus additional for deep frying

2 onions

$^1/_2$ pound/225g carrots

$^1/_2$ pound/225g Savoy cabbage

1 tablespoon sesame oil

$2^1/_2$ cups/20 fl oz/570ml vegetable bouillon or water

2–3 tablespoons miso

1 teaspoon arrowroot

1 tablespoon water

1 Cube the tofu and deep fry until golden brown. Drain and set aside.

2 Slice the onions thinly. Chop the carrots and cabbage. Sauté the vegetables in the oil for a minute or two. Add the deep-fried tofu cubes and the bouillon or water. Bring to a boil, cover and reduce the heat. Leave to simmer for about 10 minutes.

3 Remove a little of the hot liquid and use it to cream the miso before stirring it into the saucepan. Dissolve the arrowroot in the tablespoon of water and stir into the saucepan until thickened.

Tofu and Green Pea Bhajia

IN INDIA A BLAND CHEESE CALLED PANIR IS OFTEN SERVED CUBED AND FRIED. TOFU WORKS
BEAUTIFULLY IN ITS PLACE. SERVE THIS WITH BASMATI RICE, CHUTNEY AND PAPPADUMS OR CHAPATIS.

2 cups/1 pound/455g tofu

2 onions

2 tablespoons vegetable oil

3 tomatoes

2 cloves garlic

2 fresh chilies

$\frac{1}{2}$ in/1.5cm fresh ginger

2 teaspoons coriander seeds

2 teaspoons turmeric

$\frac{1}{4}$ teaspoon chili powder

A little sea salt

$1\frac{1}{3}$ cups/$\frac{1}{2}$ pound/225g fresh or
   frozen peas

1 Cut the tofu into small cubes. Deep fry them until lightly
   golden. Drain well.

2 Chop the onions. Fry in the vegetable oil for about
   3 minutes.

3 Chop the tomatoes. Mince the garlic. De-seed and finely
   chop the chilies. Peel and finely chop the ginger. Add the
   ingredients with the coriander, turmeric, and chili powder to
   the onion and stir well. Cook for about 5 minutes.

4 Add the fried tofu cubes to the saucepan. Sprinkle a little
   salt over them and stir well. Cover the pan and cook for
   2–3 minutes.

5 Add the peas to the saucepan (if they are frozen the heat
   may need to be turned up briefly). Cover and cook until
   they are tender, 3–4 minutes.

Tofu "Scrambled Eggs"

MASHED TOFU HAS A CONSISTENCY REMARKABLY LIKE SCRAMBLED EGGS. HERE IS A BASIC VERSION.
SERVE ON WHOLE-WHEAT TOAST. A QUICK RECIPE.

2 cups/1 pound/455g tofu

2 tablespoons vegetable oil

$\frac{1}{2}$ teaspoon onion salt

1 tablespoon soy sauce

$\frac{1}{2}$ teaspoon turmeric

Soy bakon bits as required (optional)

1 Mash the tofu and combine with the rest of the ingredients,
   except the oil.

2 Heat the oil and add the tofu mixture. Stir well over a high
   heat until well heated.

Scrambled Tofu and Mushrooms

THIS IS ANOTHER SIMPLE TOFU SCRAMBLE. SERVE ON TOAST. A QUICK RECIPE.

4 cups/½ pound/225g mushrooms

3 tablespoons vegetable oil

2 cups/1 pound/455g tofu

3 teaspoons turmeric

4 teaspoons prepared mustard

2 teaspoons garlic salt

Freshly ground black pepper
    as required

4 scallions

1 Chop the mushrooms finely. Sauté in the oil until tender.

2 Mash the tofu in a bowl. Add the turmeric, mustard, garlic salt, and pepper and mix well.

3 Add the tofu mixture to the mushrooms and stir over a medium heat until well heated.

4 Chop the scallions finely and stir into the tofu. Serve everything piping hot.

Tofu Knishes

THIS IS ANOTHER "SCRAMBLED" TOFU RECIPE; BUT IN THIS ONE THE TOFU RESEMBLES COTTAGE CHEESE RATHER THAN EGGS. SERVE WITH SALAD OR COOKED VEGETABLES.

2 cups/½ pound/225g whole-wheat
flour

2 teaspoons baking powder

Pinch of sea salt

1 tablespoon soy flour

5 oz/140g vegan margarine

½ cup/4 fl oz/125ml soy milk

4 large or 6–8 small scallions

1½ cups/¾ pound/340g tofu

4 tablespoons soy yogurt

Sea salt as required

1 Combine the flour, baking powder, salt, and soy flour in a large bowl. Cut in ½ cup/4 oz/115g margarine then add the milk and mix well. Chill the dough for an hour or more.

2 Chop the scallions finely. Sauté in the remainder of the margarine in a skillet until beginning to brown.

3 Put the tofu into a dish towel and squeeze the moisture out of it. Transfer it to a mixing bowl, and stir in the yogurt and a little salt. Add the sautéed scallions.

4 Roll the dough about ⅛ inch/3mm thick on a lightly floured surface. Cut into 3-inch/7.5cm circles. Place about a tablespoon of the tofu mixture on each; fold the dough over and pinch the edges together. Place on an oiled baking sheet and bake at 350°F/180°C/Gas Mark 4 for about half an hour.

Tofu Burgers

ANOTHER USE FOR MASHED TOFU IS TO MAKE BURGERS. SERVE THEM IN WHOLE-WHEAT BUNS WITH ANY DESIRED ACCOMPANIMENTS. A QUICK RECIPE.

1½ cups/¾ pound/340g tofu

½ cup/2 oz/55g whole-wheat flour

½ cup/2 oz/55g soy flour

3 teaspoons miso

1 onion

2 tablespoons vegetable oil plus additional for shallow-frying burgers

OPTIONAL ACCOMPANIMENTS

lettuce or alfalfa sprouts and sliced tomatoes or ketchup

1 Drain the tofu well. Mash in a bowl. Add the flours and the miso.

2 Chop the onion finely. Sauté in the 2 tablespoons oil until lightly browned.

3 Add the onions to the tofu mixture in the flour, mixing thoroughly to ensure that the miso is well spread through the mixture. Form into four burgers.

4 Shallow fry in a little more oil, turning once, until well-browned on both sides.

Savory Tofu Mince

SERVE OVER BROWN RICE OR PASTA, OR WITH MASHED POTATOES.

2 cups/1 pound/455g frozen tofu

1 large onion

3 sticks celery

2 carrots

2 cups/15 fl oz/425ml water

2–3 teaspoons yeast extract

3–4 teaspoons curry powder

⅙ cup/1 oz/30g raisins

1 Defrost the tofu and squeeze out as much moisture as possible.

2 Chop the onion, celery, and carrot finely. Place in a saucepan.

3 Crumble the tofu into the saucepan. Add the water and bring to a boil. Stir in the yeast extract, curry powder, and raisins. Lower the heat and simmer for about 15 minutes.

Crispy Fried Sea-flavor Frozen Tofu

FROZEN TOFU CAN ALSO BE USED TO MAKE A "FISHY" DISH LIKE THIS ONE, FLAVORED WITH A SEA VEGETABLE. IF DESIRED, SERVE WITH SLICES OF LEMON AND VEGAN TARTARE SAUCE, AND SEASONAL VEGETABLES OR SALAD. A QUICK RECIPE.

2–3 cups/1–1½ pounds/455–650g frozen tofu which has been sliced into 12–16 slices before freezing
2½ cups/20 fl oz/570ml boiling water
4 tablespoons soy sauce
1 oz/30g kombu
¾ cup/3 oz/85g cornmeal
2 teaspoons kelp powder
Vegetable oil as required

1 Put the frozen tofu slices in a large container. Pour in the boiling water; add the soy sauce and kombu. Cover the container and leave it for about 10 minutes, then put it in a cool room or refrigerator to marinate for at least an hour or two (this can be done in the morning and the marinade left in the refrigerator all day).

2 Spread the cornmeal out on a plate and mix in the kelp powder.

3 Remove the tofu slices from the marinade. (The kombu itself is not used in this dish but can be added to any other dish that requires pre-soaked kombu; the marinade itself can also be used in a soup, stew, or gravy.) Squeeze the slices very gently, then place on the plate with the cornmeal mixture and coat them thoroughly on both sides.

4 Shallow fry the slices in oil on each side until lightly browned.

Tofu Goulash

THIS RECIPE WAS FORMULATED SPECIFICALLY FOR DRIED TOFU. SERVE IT OVER NOODLES.

5 oz/140g dried-frozen tofu

2 onions

1 large or 2 small green bell peppers

3 tablespoons vegetable oil

2 tablespoons whole-wheat flour plus
   additional for coating

3 teaspoons paprika

$^{1}/_{2}$ pound/225g tomatoes

$2^{1}/_{2}$ cups/20 fl oz/570ml water

3 teaspoons yeast extract

3 tablespoons tomato paste

Freshly ground black pepper
   as required

Whole-wheat noodles as required

1 Rehydrate the tofu.

2 Chop the onions and bell pepper. Sauté in the oil for
   3–4 minutes.

3 Squeeze excess liquid from the tofu and cut into 1
   inch/2.5cm cubes. Spread some flour on a plate and roll the
   cubes in this. Add the cubes to the saucepan and stir well for
   about 2 minutes.

4 Sprinkle in the paprika and the flour, and stir for another
   2 minutes.

5 Chop the tomatoes coarsely (peeled if desired). Add them to
   the saucepan together with the water, yeast extract, tomato
   paste, and pepper. Bring to a boil, lower the heat, cover and
   simmer for about 15 minutes, stirring occasionally. Serve
   over cooked noodles.

Smoked Tofu Stew

SMOKED TOFU ADDS A LOVELY FLAVOR TO A TRADITIONAL STEW. SERVE IT WITH WARM, CRUSTY BREAD.

1 onion

2 sticks celery

1 large or 2 small carrots

3 cups/6 oz/170g mushrooms

3/4–1 pound/340–455g potatoes

1 cup/1/2 pound/225g smoked tofu

3 tablespoons vegetable oil

2 cups/15 fl oz/425ml vegetable
   bouillon or water

2 teaspoons yeast extract

2–3 bay leaves

2 tablespoons water

2 tablespoons whole-wheat flour

Sea salt as required

Freshly ground black pepper
   as required

1 Chop the onion, celery, carrot, mushrooms, and potatoes. Dice the tofu. Heat the oil in a large saucepan and sauté the vegetables and tofu for a few minutes.

2 Pour in the bouillon, stir in the yeast extract, and add the bay leaves. Bring to a boil, then lower the heat, cover and cook for about 45 minutes.

3 Stir the flour into the water, then stir this into the saucepan. Season to taste and serve.

Smoked Tofu Pasties

SMOKED TOFU MAKES A GOOD FILLING FOR PASTIES. SERVE THEM WITH COOKED VEGETABLES OR SALAD.

1 cup/¹/₂ pound/225g smoked tofu

¹/₂ pound/225g tomatoes

3 onions

1 teaspoon mixed herbs

Sea salt as required

Freshly ground black pepper
   as required

³/₄ pound/340g Whole-wheat Pastry
   (see page 65)

1 Chop the smoked tofu into small cubes. Peel and chop the tomatoes. Peel and chop the onions. Mix together in a bowl, along with the herbs and salt and pepper to taste.

2 Divide the pastry into 8 portions. Roll each one out and spoon some of the tofu mixture on to half; fold over and place on a baking sheet.

3 When all the pasties have been filled and folded, score the tops lightly with a knife or prick them with a fork. Bake at 425°F/220°C/Gas Mark 7 for 20 minutes, then lower the heat and bake for another half hour at 350°F/180°C/Gas Mark 4.

Smoked Tofu Charlotte

THIS IS QUITE A LIGHT DISH, SO SERVE IT WITH BAKED OR ROAST POTATOES.

4 cups/¹/₂ pound/225g mushrooms

5 sticks celery

¹/₄ cup/2¹/₂ oz/70g plus 1 tablespoon
   vegan margarine

³/₄ cup/6 oz/170g smoked tofu

2 tablespoons vegetable oil

¹/₂ cup/2 oz/55g whole-wheat flour

2 cups/15 fl oz/425ml soy milk

Sea salt as required

Freshly ground black pepper as required

2 cups/4 oz/115g whole-wheat
   bread crumbs

1 Chop the mushrooms and celery. Sauté them in ¹/₄ cup/2 oz/55g margarine for a few minutes.

2 Dice the smoked tofu and sauté in the oil in a skillet at the same time.

3 Stir the flour into the mushrooms and celery, cook for about a minute, then gradually stir in the milk. Stir until thickened, then season. Stir in the tofu.

4 Transfer to an oiled baking dish and top with bread crumbs. Sprinkle shavings of the remaining margarine on top and bake at 375°F/175°C/Gas Mark 5 for 15–20 minutes.

Leek and Smoked Tofu Au Gratin

THIS RECIPE, IDEAL FOR A LIGHT LUNCH, IS BEST WITH BOILED NEW POTATOES.

8 leeks

1 cup/$^{1}/_{2}$ pound/225g smoked tofu

$^{1}/_{4}$ cup/2 oz/55g vegan margarine

2 tablespoons vegetable oil

$^{1}/_{3}$ cup/1$^{1}/_{2}$ oz/45g whole-wheat flour

2$^{1}/_{2}$ cups/20 fl oz/570ml soy milk

1 cup/4 oz/115g any vegan hard
   cheese, grated

Sea salt as required

Freshly ground black pepper
   as required

1 cup/2 oz/55g fresh bread crumbs

1 Trim and wash the leeks and chop them coarsely. Cook in a small amount of lightly salted boiling water until tender. Drain.

2 Meanwhile, dice the tofu and sauté in the oil until lightly browned.

3 Melt the margarine in a saucepan and stir in the flour. Cook for a minute and then gradually stir in the milk. Bring to a boil, stirring constantly. Now stir in about three-quarters of the cheese. Taste and add additional seasoning if required.

4 Place the cooked leeks and sautéed tofu in a shallow ovenproof dish and pour the sauce over them. Top with the bread crumbs and the remainder of the cheese. Place under a moderate broiler until nicely browned. Serve immediately.

Tempeh Croquettes with Mushroom Sauce

SERVE THIS DELICIOUS DISH WITH DELICATE VEGETABLES SUCH AS SNOW PEAS. SUITABLE FOR A DINNER PARTY.

2 cups/1 pound/455g tempeh

¼ cup/2 oz/55g vegetable margarine

½ cup/2 oz/55g whole-wheat flour

1⅓ cups/10 fl oz/285ml soy milk

2 scallions

2 tablespoons soy flour

1 tablespoon soy sauce

3 teaspoons lemon juice

Sea salt as required

Freshly ground black pepper as required

2 tablespoons chick pea flour

4 tablespoons water

2 cups/4 oz/115g fresh bread crumbs

Oil for deep frying as required

FOR THE SAUCE

2 cups/4 oz/115g mushrooms

2 tablespoons vegetable oil

3 tablespoons whole-wheat flour

1 cup/8 fl oz/225ml water

1–2 teaspoons miso

1 Steam the tempeh for about 15 minutes. Set aside.

2 Heat the margarine, stir in the flour, then gradually stir in the milk, stirring constantly to avoid lumps. When the sauce has thickened remove it from the heat and mash the tempeh in it. Return to the heat and stir well for another minute. Remove from heat.

3 Chop the scallions finely and add to the mixture. Stir in the soy flour, soy sauce, lemon juice, and seasoning. Spread out on a plate to cool, then shape into croquettes.

4 Beat the chick pea flour into the water with a fork. Dip the croquettes into the bread crumbs, then into the flour mixture, and then once again into the bread crumbs. Leave the croquettes for two hours or longer, to allow them to dry out so that the bread crumbs will adhere to them when deep fried.

5 When ready to serve, just heat up the oil and deep-fry the croquettes until nicely browned.

6 To make the sauce, chop the mushrooms and sauté them in the oil until tender. Stir in the flour, then gradually add the water, stirring constantly to avoid lumps. When boiling and thickening, lower the heat and stir in the miso (softened, if necessary in a little hot water).

Smoked Tofu and Mashed Potato Cakes

IF YOU STILL HAVE AN OLD-FASHIONED MEAT MINCER THEN USE IT FOR THIS DISH. WITH LEFTOVER POTATOES IT TAKES NO TIME AT ALL TO MAKE. SERVE WITH SALAD OR COOKED SEASONAL VEGETABLES. A QUICK RECIPE.

1 pound/455g potatoes
2 cups/1 pound/455g smoked tofu
2 tablespoons minced parsley
1–2 tablespoons grated onion
Freshly ground black pepper
   as required
Whole-wheat flour as required
Vegetable oil for frying as required

1　Cook the potatoes until tender, then cool, peel, and mash.
2　Mash the tofu or put it through a mincer.
3　Combine the mashed potato, tofu, parsley, onion, and pepper and form into patties. Dip them lightly, on both sides, in the flour.
4　Shallow fry the cakes on both sides until nicely browned.

Indonesian-style Tempeh

TEMPEH HAS ITS ORIGINS IN INDONESIA, AND THIS RECIPE INCORPORATES SOME TRADITIONAL FLAVORS FROM THAT PART OF THE WORLD. SERVE IT OVER BROWN RICE. (LOVERS OF SPICY FOOD COULD SERVE SAMBAL OELEK WITH THIS, AN INDONESIAN CHILI RELISH FOUND AT MANY DELICATESSENS.)

1½ cups/¾ pound/340g tempeh
½ pound/225g potatoes
2 teaspoons coriander seeds
1 onion
1 clove garlic
2 tablespoons vegetable oil
1 teaspoon turmeric
1 teaspoon sea salt
1 teaspoon raw cane sugar
1 teaspoon lemon juice
1 teaspoon finely grated fresh ginger
2½ cups/20 fl oz/570ml water
1 cup/4 oz/115g cabbage
1 oz/30g creamed coconut
Brown rice as required

1 Cut the tempeh into cubes. Cut the potatoes into small pieces and set aside.

2 Grind the coriander seeds. Grate the onion. Mince the garlic.

3 Heat the vegetable oil in a large saucepan. Add the coriander, turmeric, onion, garlic, salt, sugar, lemon juice, and ginger. Stir for a minute. Add the tempeh and potatoes and stir for another minute or two. Add the water, bring to a boil, lower the heat, cover and simmer for about 10 minutes.

4 Shred the cabbage. Grate or finely chop the creamed coconut. Add these ingredients to the saucepan. Cover and cook for 5–10 minutes until the potatoes are thoroughly cooked.

Tempeh Stroganoff

IN THIS DISH TEMPEH IS THE "MEAT" AND TOFU PROVIDES THE "CREAM". SERVE IT OVER NOODLES.

2 cloves garlic

4 tablespoons vegetable oil

3 tablespoons soy sauce

²/₃ cup/5 fl oz/140ml apple juice

¹/₂ teaspoon ground ginger

¹/₂ teaspoon paprika

Freshly ground black pepper
  as required

2 cups/1 pound/455g tempeh

6 cups/³/₄ pound/340g mushrooms

2 tablespoons vegan margarine

¹/₂ teaspoon dried basil

A little freshly grated nutmeg

1 cup/¹/₂ pound/225g tofu

Juice of 1 small lemon

1 Mince the garlic. Combine 2 tablespoons oil, the soy sauce, apple juice, ginger, paprika, pepper, and the garlic in a large saucepan. Cube the tempeh. Add to the mixture in the saucepan and cook over a low heat for about 5 minutes, stirring occasionally.

2 Slice the mushrooms. Melt the margarine in a skillet and add the mushrooms. Sprinkle in the basil and a little grated nutmeg. Stir over a medium to low heat for about 5 minutes until tender. Add the mushrooms to the tempeh and stir well.

3 Put the tofu, remaining 2 tablespoons oil, and lemon juice in a liquidizer and blend thoroughly. Add the mixture to the tempeh and mushroom mixture and heat over a low heat until it is warmed through.

Tempeh Burgers

STEAMING TEMPEH IN A TASTY SAUCE GIVES A LOVELY FLAVOR WITH NO GREAT EFFORT. SERVE WITH LETTUCE AND/OR ONION IF DESIRED. A QUICK RECIPE.

2 cups/1 pound/455g tempeh

1½ cups/12 fl oz/340ml tomato ketchup

4 tablespoons cider vinegar or wine vinegar

8 tablespoons water

1 tablespoon soy sauce

Good pinch of black pepper

Good pinch of cayenne pepper

Lettuce (optional)

Sliced raw onion (optional)

1 If the tempeh is frozen, defrost it. Cut it into 4 pieces.

2 Put the ketchup, vinegar, water, soy sauce, and seasoning into a saucepan. Bring to a boil.

3 Place the tempeh in the saucepan, cover and lower heat to simmer. Cook on one side for 5–7 minutes, then turn over and cook on the other side for 5–7 minutes.

4 Leave to cool. (If desired, this may be left in the refrigerator until meal-time.)

5 Heat a broiler to moderately hot and place the tempeh under it. Cook on one side for 5–10 minutes until well cooked, then turn over, spreading any remaining sauce over the top half of the tempeh, and broil the other half for the same amount of time.

Classic Dishes

When we think of our favorite foods we think of the international classics – Italian, Mexican, Chinese, and good ol' American cooking. We always come back to these time tested recipes because they're simply delicious! Of course not many of the recipes we think of as classics were originally vegan dishes, so it can sometimes feel like you'll be deprived of old friends if you change to a meat- and dairy-free diet.

That's why this selection is so special. We've recreated your favorite tastes and flavors from around the world, and from home too, so you know you can eat a nutritious, low-fat healthy meal without feeling like you're missing out.

Mexican Classics

Hot and spicy, Mexican and Tex Mex dishes are always fun to eat. What's more, it is very easy to turn traditional dishes into vegan classics!

Chili con Tofu

SERVE THIS CHILI WITH RICE OR AS A FILLING FOR TACOS. MAKE SURE YOU USE MEXICAN CHILI SEASONING, WHICH CAN BE FOUND AT MOST SUPERMARKETS, AND NOT CHILI POWDER.

2 onions
2 tablespoons vegetable oil
2 cans (14–16 oz/400g each) kidney beans
1 cup/½ pound/225g firm tofu
Mexican chili seasoning as required
⅔ cup/5 oz/140g tomato paste
2 cups/4 oz/115g whole-wheat bread crumbs

1 Chop the onions and fry in the oil until lightly browned. Drain the kidney beans.
2 Put the tofu into a clean dish towel and squeeze as much of the liquid out as possible so that the tofu is quite dry and crumbly.
3 Combine all of the ingredients in a saucepan, adding enough water to make the mixture stirrable. Bring to a boil over a moderate heat, stirring constantly; turn the heat to low and simmer for about 10 minutes.

Quick and Easy Chili

THE CHILI SEASONING CALLED FOR IN THIS RECIPE IS THE MIXTURE OF MEXICAN CHILI SPICES BY MCCORMICKS AND OTHERS, AVAILABLE AT MANY SUPERMARKETS. A QUICK RECIPE.

1 large onion
4 tablespoons vegetable oil
½ pound/225g bulgur wheat
2 cans (14–16 oz/400g each) tomatoes
Sea salt as required
1 teaspoon chili seasoning or to taste
2½ cups/1 pound/455g or 2 cans (14–16 oz/400g each) cooked drained kidney beans

1 Chop the onion and sauté it in the oil until it begins to soften.
2 Add the bulgur wheat and cook for 2–3 minutes more, stirring constantly.
3 Add the cans of tomatoes and some more water if needed (the liquid should be about three times the volume of the bulgur wheat). Add the seasoning and the cooked beans.
4 Simmer until tender – about 15 minutes.

Chili con Elote

"ELOTE" MEANS MAIZE IN SPANISH, AND THE COMBINATION OF BEANS AND MAIZE IS A TRADITIONAL
MEXICAN ONE. THIS IS GOOD WITH FLOUR TORTILLAS.

2 onions

2 cloves garlic

3 tablespoons vegetable oil

2 small or 1 large green bell pepper

1⅓ cups/10 fl oz/285ml vegetable
    bouillon

2½ tablespoons tomato paste

1⅔ cups/10 oz/285g cooked corn
    (fresh, frozen, or canned)

2½ cups/1 pound/455g or 2 cans
    (14–16 oz/400g each) cooked
    drained kidney beans

3 teaspoons Mexican chili seasoning

1 Chop the onion and garlic. Sauté in the oil until lightly
  browned.

2 Chop the bell pepper, add to the saucepan, and cook for
  another 2–3 minutes.

3 Add the bouillon and tomato paste to the saucepan and
  bring to a boil. Add the corn. Lower the heat to simmering.

4 Mash half the beans in a bowl. Add both the mashed beans
  and whole beans to the saucepan together with the
  seasoning. Stir well.

5 Simmer, uncovered, for about 15 minutes, by which time all
  the liquid should have been absorbed.

6 Serve immediately.

Enchiladas

UNDENIABLY A RATHER COMPLICATED AND ELABORATE RECIPE, BUT THE RESULTS JUSTIFY THE EFFORT. SERVE IT WITH A GREEN SALAD.

TORTILLAS

1¼ cups/5 oz/140g whole-wheat flour

½ cup/3 oz/85g cornmeal

Pinch of sea salt

5 tablespoons vegan margarine

SALSA

1 onion

2 cloves garlic

2 tablespoons vegetable oil

1 small can (about 7 oz/200g)
   tomatoes

2 tablespoons Mexican chili seasoning

Freshly ground black pepper as
   required

1 teaspoon cumin seeds

¼ teaspoon cayenne pepper

⅔ cup/5 oz/140g tomato paste

2 cups/15 fl oz/425ml water

FILLING

1½–2 cups/¾–1 pound/340–455g firm
   tofu

⅔ cup/5 fl oz/140ml soy yogurt

Sea salt as required

½ teaspoon turmeric

¼ teaspoon paprika

1 cup/2 oz/55g button mushrooms

3–4 scallions

Black olives as required

1 To make the tortillas, combine the flour and cornmeal in a bowl. Add a pinch of salt then blend in the margarine. Add enough water to form a dough. Make small balls out of the dough (the size does not matter, as you can make either small or large tortillas), and roll them out with a rolling pin on a floured board. Place each tortilla on a non-stick skillet over a moderately high heat. When it begins to bubble, turn it over until the other side begins to bubble. Remove from the heat, stack on a plate and set aside.

2 To make the salsa chop the onion and garlic finely. Sauté in the oil until softened.

3 Chop the chilies finely. Put the tomatoes and their juice into a liquidizer and blend thoroughly.

4 Add the chilies, chili seasoning, black pepper, cumin seeds, cayenne pepper, tomato paste, blended tomatoes, and water to the onion and garlic. Stir well. Bring to a boil, then simmer for about 20 minutes.

5 To make the filling mash the tofu and mix in the yogurt, salt, turmeric, and paprika.

6 Chop the mushrooms and scallions finely and add to the tofu mixture. Chop the olives and set aside.

7 To assemble the dish, brush each tortilla with a little of the salsa, then spoon a little of the filling into the center. Fold it over twice to form a rolled pancake shape. Cover the bottom of a baking dish with a thin layer of salsa and place each filled tortilla on the sheet. When all the tortillas have been filled, spoon the remaining salsa over the top. If there is any filling left it can be used as decoration over the salsa. Finally, garnish with the chopped olives.

8 Bake the enchiladas in the oven at 350°F/180°C/Gas Mark 4 for about half an hour. Serve immediately.

Tofu, Rice, and Zucchini Enchiladas

THIS ENCHILADA DISH WOULD BE A GOOD MAIN COURSE FOR A DINNER PARTY. AGAIN, A GREEN SALAD IS THE BEST ACCOMPANIMENT.

TORTILLAS

1¼ cups/5 oz/140g whole-wheat flour

½ cup/3 oz/85g cornmeal

Pinch of sea salt

5 tablespoons vegan margarine

1 cup/6 oz/170g brown rice

1 can (14–16 oz/400g) tomatoes

Mexican chili seasoning to taste

Chili powder as required (optional)

1 large onion

1 clove garlic

2 tablespoons olive oil

2 zucchini

1–1½ cups/½–¾ pound/225–340g firm tofu

2 tablespoons sesame seeds

2–3 scallions

1 Make the tortillas according to the instructions in the previous recipe.

2 Cook the rice in boiling salted water until tender and set aside. (This may be done in advance.)

3 Put the tomatoes into a liquidizer, add some chili seasoning and blend thoroughly. Taste, and if the flavor is not sufficiently strong stir in additional seasoning; if it is not spicy enough add a little chili powder. (The main constituents of Mexican chili seasoning are cumin, oregano, and chili powder; a combination of these will produce a "Mexican" flavor.)

4 Chop the onion and garlic. Sauté in the oil in a large saucepan until tender.

5 Chop the zucchini finely. Add to the onion and garlic, along with the rice. Crumble the tofu into this mixture, adding a little salt to taste. Mix thoroughly.

6 Dip each tortilla into the puréed tomatoes, then place on a baking dish that has been oiled with olive oil and place a little filling on it. Roll up to close.

7 When all the tortillas have been filled, spoon the remainder of the puréed tomatoes over the top and sprinkle with the sesame seeds. Bake in the oven at 375°F/190°C/Gas Mark 5 for about half an hour.

8 Chop the scallions finely and sprinkle over the enchiladas as garnish.

Burritos

THIS IS MORE OF AN EVERYDAY DISH THAN THE PREVIOUS TWO RECIPES.

3 cups/³/₄ pound/340g whole-wheat
  flour

1 teaspoon sea salt

1 large onion

2 cups/4 oz/115g mushrooms

2 tablespoons vegetable oil

2 cups/1 pound/455g firm tofu

3 teaspoons Mexican chili seasoning

2 tablespoons soy sauce

1 can (14–16 oz/400g) tomatoes

2 teaspoons ground cumin

¹/₂ teaspoon dried basil

2 teaspoons chopped parsley

1 Put the flour and salt in a large bowl and add enough water to make a dough. Cover with a damp cloth and leave for an hour or longer. Knead the dough, then pull off individual lumps and roll each one out into a round on a floured board. Heat a heavy skillet, and cook each round for a few minutes on each side before removing from the heat.

2 Chop the onion and mushrooms and sauté in the oil until tender. Crumble in the tofu and sprinkle with the chili seasoning. Cook for about 10 minutes longer, stirring frequently. Add the soy sauce.

3 Put the tomatoes into a liquidizer with the cumin, basil, and parsley. Blend thoroughly.

4 Add half the blended tomatoes to the tofu mixture, and stir well. Fill the burritos with this mixture and roll up. Place on an oiled baking pan and top with the rest of the tomato sauce. Bake in the oven at 350°F/180°C/Gas Mark 4 for 20–30 minutes.

Kidney Bean
Cheeseburgers
(p.234)

Tofu Guacamole (p.29), Hummus (p.29), Eggplant and Tahini Dip (p.34) served with bread and olives

Tofu Italian Pizza (p.222)

Tacos with Refried Beans (p.185)

Peanut Butter
Oaties (p.249) and
Cherry Coconut
Refrigerator
Cookies (p.250)

Raspberry Cheesecake (p.254)

Applesauce Cake with maple syrup glaze (p.275)

Summer Fruit Cup (p.281)

Rancheros

TRADITIONALLY THIS DISH IS MADE WITH SCRAMBLED EGGS, BUT IT WORKS WELL WITH TOFU. SERVE WITH BROWN RICE OR TORTILLAS.

1 can (14–16 oz/400g) tomatoes
1 onion
1 green bell pepper
1 red bell pepper
2 tablespoons vegetable oil
2 teaspoons Mexican chili seasoning
$1/2$ teaspoon turmeric
$1/4$ cup/1 oz/30g soy flour
2 cups/1 pound/455g firm tofu

1 Drain the tomatoes and discard the juice.
2 Chop the onion and bell peppers and sauté in the oil until just tender. Add the chili seasoning, turmeric, and soy flour. Stir well, then slowly add the tomatoes. Bring to a boil, lower the heat and simmer for about 5 minutes.
3 Put the tofu into a clean dish towel and squeeze well to extract the moisture.
4 Add the crumbled tofu to the tomato mixture. Heat for a minute or two before serving.

Spicy Tofu Tacos

TACO SHELLS ARE READILY AVAILABLE, AND HERE IS A QUICK AND EASY FILLING FOR THEM. THIS QUANTITY IS ENOUGH FOR A LIGHT LUNCH; FOR A FULL EVENING MEAL SERVE WITH MEXICAN RICE AND REFRIED BEANS.

1 onion
2 cloves garlic
3 tablespoons vegetable oil
1 tablespoon Mexican chili seasoning
2 tablespoons whole-wheat flour
1^1/$_3$ cups/10 fl oz/285ml water
2 tablespoons tomato paste
1 teaspoon yeast extract
1 cup/^{1}/$_2$ pound/225g firm tofu
Sea salt as required
Freshly ground black pepper
  as required
1 package (12) taco shells
Lettuce as required

1 Chop the onion and mince the garlic. Sauté in the oil for a few minutes until tender. Stir in the chili seasoning and the flour. Add the water slowly, stirring constantly until it comes to a boil. Stir in the tomato paste and the yeast extract.

2 Crumble the tofu into the sauce. Simmer, uncovered, for about 10 minutes or until thick. Taste and add salt and pepper if required.

3 Meanwhile, heat the tacos according to the instructions on the package.

4 Fill the taco shells with the tofu mixture and top with shredded lettuce.

Tacos with Refried Beans

2 onions

3–4 cloves garlic

3 tablespoons vegetable oil

2½ cups/1 pound/455g or 2 cans
(14–16 oz/400g each) cooked
kidney beans

2 tablespoons Mexican chili seasoning
or to taste

1 package (12) taco shells

OPTIONAL EXTRAS

Shredded lettuce, grated vegan hard
cheese, vegan sour cream

1 Chop the onion. Mince the garlic. Heat the oil in a saucepan
and sauté them until tenderized.

2 Drain the beans, retaining a little of the liquid from the can,
and rinse them. Add them to the saucepan, along with a
little of the liquid from the can and the chili seasoning. Stir
well for a minute or two, then mash the beans with a fork,
potato masher, or pastry blender (they do not have to be
particularly smooth). Continue cooking for a few minutes,
stirring frequently.

3 Heat the taco shells. Divide the bean mixture between the
shells, top with optional extras and serve immediately.

Hot Chili Guacamole

THIS SIMPLE GUACAMOLE CAN BE SERVED AS AN ACCOMPANIMENT TO OTHER MEXICAN DISHES OR
AS A TOPPING.

1 cup/½ pound/225g soft or
medium tofu

2 large tomatoes

1 small onion

2 cloves garlic

2 fresh chilies

3 ripe avocados

Juice of ½ lemon

Sea salt as required

1 Place the tofu in a liquidizer and blend. Set aside.

2 Peel and dice the tomatoes. Chop the onion, garlic, and
chilies very finely.

3 Peel and mash the avocados. Add all the rest of the
ingredients and mix thoroughly. Serve immediately.

Tamale Pie

RECIPES WITH A LONG LIST OF INGREDIENTS CAN LOOK INTIMIDATING, BUT THIS ONE IS REALLY VERY SIMPLE AND DOES NOT TAKE LONG AT ALL. SERVE WITH A FRESH GREEN SALAD.

2½ cups/1 pound/225g or 2 cans (16 oz/425g each) cooked drained pinto beans

2 onions

3 tablespoons vegetable oil

3 cloves garlic

1 small green bell pepper

3 sticks celery

½ teaspoon chili powder (or to taste)

2 teaspoons ground cumin

2 teaspoons dried oregano

12 black olives

6 oz/170g corn (fresh, frozen, or canned)

2 tablespoons tomato paste

2 tablespoons chopped parsley

4 tablespoons water

Sea salt as required

Freshly ground black pepper as required

1½ cups/6 oz/170g cornmeal

2½ cups/20 fl oz/570ml water

Pinch of sea salt

2 tablespoons/1 oz/30g vegan margarine

4 tablespoons nutritional yeast

1 Drain the beans, mash them, and set aside.

2 Chop the onion and sauté it in the oil in a large saucepan for a few minutes.

3 Mince the garlic. Chop the bell pepper and celery. Add these ingredients to the pan and cook for a few minutes longer.

4 Add the spices to the pan. Chop the olives and add them, as well as the mashed beans, corn, tomato paste, parsley, water, and seasoning. Cook over a low heat for several minutes.

5 In another pan stir the cornmeal and salt into the water, using a whisk if necessary. Bring to a boil, stirring constantly, until it thickens and comes to a boil. Stir in the margarine and yeast.

6 Oil a baking dish and spread about two-thirds of the cornmeal mixture on the bottom. Spoon the bean mixture over this and top with the remaining cornmeal. Bake at 350°F/180°C/Gas Mark 4 for about half an hour.

Smoky Pasta and Beans

SMOKED TOFU CAN ALSO BE USED FOR DISHES FROM THIS PART OF THE WORLD. SERVE WITH A SALAD.

2½ cups/10 oz/285g whole-wheat macaroni or other pasta shape

1–1¼ cups/8–10 oz/225–285g smoked tofu

4 cloves garlic

2 tablespoons vegetable oil

2 cans (14–16 oz/400g each) kidney beans

1 tablespoon ground cumin

Freshly ground black pepper as required

Sea salt as required

1 Cook the pasta in salted boiling water until tender.

2 Meanwhile, dice the smoked tofu finely. Chop the garlic very finely. Fry in the oil in a skillet over a medium heat until the tofu is lightly browned.

3 Drain the kidney beans, retaining about 2 tablespoons of the liquid.

4 When the pasta is cooked drain it well. Put it back in the saucepan, along with the tofu and garlic, beans, bean liquid, cumin, and black pepper (additional salt should not be necessary, but add a little sea salt if required). Mix well, then cook for 4–5 minutes over a very low heat before serving.

Mexican Potato Salad

IT IS BETTER TO USE FRESHLY COOKED POTATOES FOR THIS SO THAT THE VINAIGRETTE CAN SOAK INTO THEM, BUT YOU CAN USE LEFTOVER POTATOES IF YOU PREFER.

1 pound/455g new potatoes

1 tablespoon vegetable oil

1 tablespoon cider vinegar or wine vinegar

1 can (12 oz/340g) corn

⅔ cup/5 fl oz/140ml soy yogurt

Sea salt as required

Freshly ground black pepper as required

1 bunch watercress

2 tablespoons soy bakon bits

1 Cook the potatoes until tender, drain and dice them.

2 Combine the oil and vinegar, pour this over the diced potatoes and leave until cold.

3 Drain the corn and mix it with the yogurt and seasoning. Combine this with the potatoes.

4 Pile on to a serving dish and surround with sprigs of watercress. Sprinkle soy bakon bits over the salad just before serving.

Chinese & Far Eastern Classics

These dishes are inspired by recipes from all around the Far East from Malaysia and Indonesia to Japan, China, and Korea. Being naturally low in saturated fats, and with a fantastic range of superb tofu-based dishes, Far Eastern cooking one of the healthiest options you can take.

Tofu lo Mein

FOR THOSE WHO AVOID EGGS, IT IS BECOMING MUCH EASIER THESE DAYS TO FIND EGGLESS CHINESE NOODLES (INCLUDING WHOLE-WHEAT VARIETIES) — OR THIN ITALIAN PASTA COULD BE USED INSTEAD.

1 cup/$\frac{1}{2}$ pound/225g firm tofu

1–2 tablespoons soy sauce

1–2 tablespoons cornstarch

$\frac{3}{4}$ pound/340g thin Chinese noodles

Sesame oil as required

1 can (14–16 oz/400g) bamboo shoots

1 small bunch scallions

2 tablespoons vegetable oil

$\frac{1}{2}$ pound/225g fresh bean sprouts

Sea salt as required

1 Cut the tofu into cubes. Sprinkle with the soy sauce and then with the cornstarch and toss well. Set aside.

2 Cook the noodles in salted boiling water until just tender, drain well and run cold water over them. Toss with 1 tablespoon sesame oil and set aside.

3 Drain the bamboo shoots and slice thinly. Chop the scallions.

4 Heat the vegetable oil in a wok or skillet. Add the tofu and stir-fry for 2–3 minutes. Add the bamboo shoots, lower the heat to medium and stir-fry for 1–2 minutes. Add the noodles, raise the heat and cook, stirring constantly, allowing some of the noodles to become browned.

5 Add the bean sprouts and stir-fry for 2 minutes. Add the salt, scallions, and additional sesame oil to taste and mix thoroughly. Serve immediately.

Burmese Kung to Mein

HERE IS A SPICY VERSION OF THE PREVIOUS RECIPE.

1 cup/½ pound/225g firm or
   medium tofu

4 tablespoons vegetable oil plus
   additional for deep-frying

4 cloves garlic

1 teaspoon sesame oil

½ pound/225g spinach

½ pound/225g Chinese cabbage

4 scallions

2 fresh chilies

1½–2 tablespoons soy sauce

¾ pound/340g Chinese noodles

1 Cut the tofu into cubes and deep-fry in the vegetable oil until golden. Drain and set aside.

2 Chop the garlic finely. Heat the 4 tablespoons vegetable oil and the sesame oil in a wok or large skillet until very hot. Drop in the garlic pieces and fry until brown, being careful not to let them burn. Remove and drain on kitchen towels.

3 Chop the spinach and Chinese cabbage coarsely. Chop the scallions and de-seed and chop the chilies finely. Put the vegetables into the wok and stir-fry for about 3 minutes, until the spinach has wilted. Add the deep-fried tofu and the soy sauce and mix well.

4 Cook the noodles in salted boiling water until just tender then drain. Toss with the tofu and vegetable mixture. Sprinkle with the crisp garlic bits and serve.

Nori Special Fried Rice

MASHED TOFU ADDS A SCRAMBLED EGG TEXTURE, DEEP-FRIED TOFU A CHEWY TEXTURE, AND NORI GIVES A FLAVOR OF THE SEA TO THIS DISH. A QUICK RECIPE.

$1^{1}/_{2}$–2 cups/10–12 oz/285–340g
  brown rice

2 sheets nori

3 cups/$1^{1}/_{2}$ pound/680g tofu

4–6 scallions

2 cloves garlic

$^{1}/_{2}$ inch/2.5cm piece fresh ginger

2 tablespoons vegetable oil

Soy sauce as required

Freshly ground black pepper
  as required

1–2 teaspoons sesame oil

1 Cook the rice until tender (or use leftover cooked rice). Toast the nori.

2 Dice half the tofu and deep-fry the diced tofu until golden. Mash the remainder of the tofu in a bowl.

3 Chop the scallions, garlic, and ginger very finely. Heat the vegetable oil in a wok and stir-fry these ingredients for 2–3 minutes.

4 Add the cooked rice and mashed tofu to the wok and continue stir-frying for about 2–3 minutes.

5 Add the deep-fried tofu cubes, soy sauce, and pepper. Then tear the nori into pieces and add them to the mixture. Stir well for about a minute longer, then sprinkle in the sesame oil and serve piping hot.

Tempeh Tofu Stir Fry Rice

2 cups/$^{3}/_{4}$ pound/340g brown rice

$^{3}/_{4}$ pound/340g tempeh

2 tablespoons vegetable oil plus
  additional for deep-frying

1 cup/$^{1}/_{2}$ pound/225g firm or medium
  tofu

2 teaspoons turmeric

4 scallions

2 cloves garlic

2 tablespoons soy sauce

1 Cook the rice in salted boiling water until tender.

2 Cut the tempeh into cubes and deep-fry in the oil. Drain and set aside.

3 Mash the tofu with the turmeric. Chop the scallions finely.

4 Chop the garlic finely. Heat the 2 tablespoons oil in a wok or skillet and add the garlic. Stir-fry for 30 seconds or so until lightly browned.

5 Add all the rest of the ingredients and stir-fry until everything is sizzling hot. Serve immediately.

Yellow Bean Spinach

ONCE A SPECIALIST INGREDIENT, YELLOW BEAN SAUCE IS NOW FOUND IN MOST SUPERMARKETS. IT DOES ADD A SPECIAL TANG TO THE DISH. SERVE WITH RICE OR NOODLES.

2½–3 cups/1¼–1½ pound/565–680g medium tofu

5 tablespoons vegetable oil

4 small or 2 large leeks

1 pound/455g fresh spinach

1 tablespoon cider vinegar or wine vinegar

1 tablespoon soy sauce

¼–½ teaspoon Tabasco sauce

1 tablespoon yellow bean sauce

1 Cut the tofu into small dice. Heat 3 tablespoons of the oil in a wok or skillet and, when hot, add the tofu pieces. Stir-fry for about 2 minutes, then transfer from the pan to paper towels to drain.

2 Chop the leeks and spinach. Add the rest of the oil to the pan and add the vegetables. Stir-fry for about 3 minutes.

3 Stir in the vinegar, soy sauce, Tabasco sauce, and yellow bean sauce. Add the tofu pieces and stir gently.

4 Serve with brown rice or noodles.

Syechwan Tofu

THIS RECIPE ALSO REQUIRES YELLOW BEAN SAUCE, BUT IT IS A MUCH SPICIER DISH THAN THE PREVIOUS ONE. SERVE WITH BROWN RICE. SOY SAUCE MAY BE ADDED TO THIS DISH IF DESIRED, BUT YELLOW BEAN SAUCE IS SO SALTY IT ISN'T USUALLY NECESSARY.

2 cups/1 pound/455g medium tofu
3 tablespoons vegetable oil
2 green bell peppers
2 leeks
2 fresh chilies
1–1½ teaspoons chili powder
1 tablespoon cider vinegar or wine
　　vinegar
1 teaspoon raw cane sugar
2–3 tablespoons yellow bean sauce
2 teaspoons sesame oil

1　Cut the tofu into small cubes. Heat 2 tablespoons of the oil in a wok or skillet and stir-fry the tofu cubes for 2–3 minutes. Remove from the pan and drain.

2　Slice the bell peppers into strips. Chop the leeks. De-seed and chop the chilies finely.

3　Heat the remaining oil and add the vegetables. Stir-fry for about 3 minutes. Add the chili powder, vinegar, sugar, and yellow bean sauce and mix well.

4　Return the tofu cubes to the wok and stir-fry the mixture for about 3 minutes longer. Sprinkle with the sesame oil and serve immediately.

Tofu with Chili Sauce

THIS IS A WESTERNIZED ADAPTATION OF A TRADITIONAL SZECHWAN DISH. SERVE WITH BROWN RICE.

1 leek

2 cloves garlic

2 tablespoons vegetable oil

2 cups/4 oz/115g mushrooms

$^1/_2$–1 teaspoon chili powder

$^2/_3$ cup/5 fl oz/140ml water

1 tablespoon cider vinegar or wine
   vinegar

2 tablespoons tomato ketchup

1 tablespoon soy sauce

2–3 cups/1–1$^1/_2$ pound/455–680g
   medium tofu

1 tablespoon cornstarch dissolved in
   3 tablespoons water

2 scallions

1 Chop the leek and garlic finely. Heat the oil in a wok or skillet and add the leek and garlic. Stir-fry for about 30 seconds.

2 Chop the mushrooms and add to the wok. Stir-fry for 1–2 minutes.

3 Add the chili powder, water, vinegar, tomato ketchup, and soy sauce, bring to a boil and cook for another minute.

4 Dice the tofu and add to the wok. Stir in the dissolved cornstarch and stir until thickened.

5 Chop the scallions finely and sprinkle over the tofu and sauce. Serve immediately.

Syechwan Tofu Satay

SZECHWAN CUISINE IS CHARACTERIZED BY ITS FIERY FLAVOR; TO MAKE THE DISH MORE AUTHENTIC INCREASE THE AMOUNT OF CAYENNE PEPPER. SERVE WITH BROWN RICE. VEGANS WHO DO NOT EAT HONEY COULD SUBSTITUTE RAW CANE SUGAR IN THIS RECIPE.

1 carrot

1 inch/2.5cm piece fresh ginger

1 tablespoon vegetable oil

2 cups/1 pound/455g medium tofu

1 tablespoon cider vinegar or wine vinegar

1 scallion

2 tablespoons peanut butter

1/4 teaspoon cayenne pepper

2 tablespoons sesame oil

2 tablespoons honey

1 Slice the carrot into matchsticks. Peel and chop the ginger finely. Heat the vegetable oil in a wok or skillet, add the carrot and ginger and stir-fry for 2–3 minutes.

2 Cut the tofu into small pieces. Add to the wok with the vinegar. Cover and leave to simmer for about 3 minutes.

3 Chop the scallion finely and add to the wok. Turn the heat off and leave, covered, for 1–2 minutes.

4 Meanwhile, combine the peanut butter, cayenne pepper, sesame oil, and honey in a small bowl, stirring gently until smooth.

5 Add the peanut sauce to the tofu mixture and stir in well.

Mushroom-smothered Tofu

DRIED MUSHROOMS, WHICH ARE AVAILABLE AT CHINESE STORES AND MANY SUPERMARKETS, GIVE THIS DISH A RICH AND UNIQUE FLAVOR. SERVE WITH BROWN RICE.

16 dried mushrooms

2½–3 cups/1¼–1½ pound/565–680g medium tofu

1 inch/2.5cm piece fresh ginger

2 scallions

4 tablespoons vegetable oil

2 teaspoons cider vinegar or wine vinegar

3 tablespoons soy sauce

1 teaspoon raw cane sugar

1 tablespoon sesame oil

1 Cover the mushrooms with boiling water and leave to soak for an hour or more. Drain them (reserving the liquid) and squeeze gently. Remove the stalks and slice the caps.

2 Cut the tofu into squares and then cut the squares into triangles. Set aside.

3 Peel the ginger and chop it and the scallions finely. Heat the vegetable oil in a wok or skillet. Add the ginger and scallions and stir-fry for 1 minute. Add the vinegar, soy sauce, sugar, and mushroom liquid (if less than ¾ cup/7 fl oz/200ml then add water to bring it up to that amount). Bring to a boil and add the mushrooms and tofu.

4 Turn gently a few times. Lower the heat, cover and simmer for about 10 minutes, turning once halfway through. By the end of the cooking time there should be little or no liquid remaining. Add the sesame oil and serve immediately.

Moo Goo Gai Pan

THIS CHINESE DISH — SERVED WITH RICE — IS TRADITIONALLY MADE WITH CHICKEN; HERE IS A VERSION REQUIRING NO ANIMAL INGREDIENTS.

2 onions

4 sticks celery

2 cups/4 oz/115g mushrooms

1 green or red bell pepper

1 can (10 oz/275g) water chestnuts

1–1½ cups/4–6 oz/115–170g Chinese cabbage

1½–2 cups/¾–1 pound/340–455g medium or firm tofu

3 tablespoons soy sauce

1–2 oz/30–55g fresh ginger

2–3 cloves garlic

6 tablespoons vegetable oil

2 tablespoons arrowroot

2 cups/15 fl oz/425ml water

4 tablespoons cider vinegar or wine vinegar

Sea salt as required

2 cups/4 oz/115g fresh bean sprouts

1 Slice the onions thinly. Chop the celery and mushrooms; cut the bell pepper into slivers. Slice the water chestnuts and Chinese cabbage.

2 Dice the tofu. Sprinkle the soy sauce over it, put on a broiler pan and broil under a medium heat for a few minutes on each side. Set aside.

3 Peel the ginger and chop it and the garlic finely. Sauté in 4 tablespoons of the oil in a small pan over a medium heat for about 3 minutes.

4 Mix the arrowroot with 2 tablespoons of the water, the vinegar, and salt. Pour the remainder of the water over the ginger and garlic and bring to a boil. Turn down to a simmer, then slowly stir in the arrowroot mixture until thickened.

5 Heat the remaining oil in a wok or large skillet. Add the onions, celery, mushrooms, and pepper and stir-fry for about 5 minutes. Add the Chinese cabbage, water chestnuts, and bean sprouts and stir-fry for 3–5 minutes.

6 Add the tofu to the vegetable mixture and stir well. Pour over the ginger/garlic sauce and stir over a low heat until well mixed.

Foo Yung

A FOO YUNG IS TRADITIONALLY A SCRAMBLED EGG MIXTURE; MASHED TOFU MAKES A SPLENDID
CHOLESTEROL-FREE VERSION. SERVE WITH BROWN RICE, WITH ADDITIONAL SOY SAUCE IF DESIRED.

1 onion

2 scallions

4 cups/^{1}/$_2$ pound/225g mushrooms

2 tablespoons vegetable oil

1^1/$_2$–1^3/$_4$ cups/12–14 oz/340–400g firm
  or medium tofu

1 teaspoon turmeric

Sea salt as required

1 tablespoon soy sauce

^{1}/$_2$ pound/225g bean sprouts

1 Chop the onion, scallions, and mushrooms finely. Heat the
   oil in a skillet and stir-fry the vegetables until tender.

2 Mash the tofu, mix well with the turmeric and add to the
   pan, stirring well. Add the salt and soy sauce while stirring.
   Finally, add the bean sprouts and continue stir-frying until
   they are just wilted.

Sweet and Sour Tofu with Vegetables

THIS DISH CAN BE FOUND IN SOME CHINESE RESTAURANTS. SERVE IT OVER BROWN RICE. A QUICK RECIPE.

2 cups/1 pound/455g tofu

1 bunch scallions

4 tablespoons vegetable oil

1 pound/455g tomatoes

1 can (14–16 oz/400g) pineapple chunks

¾ cup/3 oz/85g almonds

2 teaspoons cornstarch

4 tablespoons soy sauce

1　Cut the tofu into small cubes. Finely chop the scallions. Sauté them both in the oil for 3 minutes.

2　Chop the tomatoes and add them to the pan. Cook for 5 minutes.

3　Drain the pineapple and add to the pan together with the whole almonds. Cook for 2–3 minutes.

4　Dissolve the cornstarch in the soy sauce and pour the mixture over the vegetables and tofu. Stir well until thickened and simmer for a minute or two.

Deep-fried, Bite-size Sweet and Sour Tofu Balls

A LOVELY COMBINATION OF FLAVORS AND TEXTURES. SERVE WITH BROWN RICE.

2 cups/1 pound/455g medium or firm tofu

$^1/_2$ teaspoon sea salt

2 tablespoons whole-wheat flour

Vegetable oil for deep-frying as required

4 oz/115g fresh or canned pineapple in its own juice

1 green bell pepper

2 scallions

5 tablespoons cider vinegar or wine vinegar

3–4 tablespoons raw cane sugar

2–3 tablespoons soy sauce

1 tablespoon cornstarch dissolved in $^3/_4$ cup/7 fl oz/200ml pineapple juice

1 If using medium tofu wrap it in a clean dish towel or paper towel and leave to drain for half an hour or more. Put the drained tofu into a mixing bowl, mash well and stir in the salt and flour. Form into small balls and deep-fry in the oil until golden brown. Drain well.

2 Chop the pineapple. Slice the bell pepper into thin slivers. Chop the scallions finely.

3 Put the vinegar, sugar, soy sauce, and cornstarch dissolved in pineapple juice into a wok or large saucepan and bring to a boil gently, stirring constantly until thickened.

4 Add the tofu balls, pineapple, bell pepper, and scallions and simmer for 2–3 minutes to heat through. Serve immediately.

Ma Po with Noodles

WHEN THIS DISH APPEARS ON THE MENU AT A CHINESE RESTAURANT IT IS NOT NORMALLY VEGETARIAN, BUT HERE IS A MEAT-FREE VERSION. TRADITIONALLY IT IS SERVED WITH RICE, THOUGH NOODLES ARE ALSO A GOOD ACCOMPANIMENT.

2 small leeks

4 cloves garlic

2 tablespoons vegetable oil

2–3 cups/1–1½ pound/455–680g
    medium tofu

1⅓ cups/10 fl oz/285ml water or
    vegetable bouillon

2 teaspoons Chinese chili sauce

2 tablespoons soy sauce

1 teaspoon freshly ground black
    pepper

½ cup/3 oz/85g soy bakon bits

¾ pound/340g Chinese noodles

1 tablespoon cornstarch dissolved in
    2 tablespoons water

1 tablespoon sesame oil

1   Chop the leeks and garlic finely. Heat the vegetable oil in a wok or skillet and stir-fry the leeks and garlic for 3–4 minutes.

2   Dice the tofu. Stir into the leeks and garlic. Add the water or bouillon, the chili sauce, soy sauce, black pepper, and soy bakon bits. Bring to a boil, then lower the heat and simmer for about 10 minutes.

3   Cook the noodles in salted boiling water until just tender then drain.

4   Add the dissolved cornstarch to the tofu mixture and stir well until thickened. Serve the noodles topped with the sauce. Sprinkle with the sesame oil before serving.

Peking Noodles

IN THIS CHINESE NOODLE DISH FROZEN TOFU ADDS A "MEATY" TEXTURE.

2 cups/1 pound/455g frozen tofu

2 teaspoons yeast extract

²/₃ cup/5 fl oz/140ml water plus
    6 tablespoons

4 scallions

¹/₂ cucumber

¹/₂ pound/225g bean sprouts

2 cloves garlic

2 tablespoons vegetable oil

3 tablespoons Hoisin sauce

2 teaspoons soy sauce

1 tablespoon cider vinegar or
    wine vinegar

³/₄ pound/340g thin noodles

1 Defrost the tofu and squeeze well. Dissolve the yeast extract in the ²/₃ cup/5 fl oz/140ml water in a small saucepan. Crumble the tofu into this and simmer for 1–2 minutes (the liquid should be completely absorbed). Set aside.

2 Chop 2 of the scallions finely. Coarsely grate the cucumber. Mix these ingredients with the bean sprouts and set aside.

3 Chop the garlic finely. Stir-fry in the oil in a wok or large skillet with the tofu for 1–2 minutes.

4 Chop the remaining 2 scallions finely and add them to the wok, along with the Hoisin sauce, soy sauce, vinegar, and 6 tablespoons water. Simmer this mixture briefly. Meanwhile, cook the noodles in salted boiling water until just tender.

5 Serve the noodles with the tofu sauce poured over them, topped with the mixture of bean sprouts, cucumber, and scallions.

Indonesian Tahu Goreng

TOFU IS KNOWN AS TAHU IN INDONESIA, WHERE IT FORMS THE MAIN INGREDIENT OF VARIOUS DISHES. GORENG JUST MEANS FRIED, AND TAHU GORENG CAN SIMPLY BE SLICES OF DEEP-FRIED TOFU OR IT CAN BE A SPICY DISH LIKE THIS ONE.

$2\frac{1}{2}$ cups/$1\frac{1}{4}$ pound/565g medium or firm tofu

Cornstarch as required

Vegetable oil for deep-frying as required

$\frac{3}{4}$ pound/340g bean sprouts

$\frac{1}{2}$ cucumber

2 fresh chilies

3 cloves garlic

3 scallions

2 tablespoons lemon juice

4 tablespoons soy sauce

1 tablespoon raw cane sugar

Cooked brown rice as required

1 Dice the tofu. Spread cornstarch out on a plate and roll the tofu cubes in it. Deep-fry the cubes in the oil and set aside (keep warm if desired).

2 Blanch the bean sprouts in boiling water for 1 minute, then drain and pour cold water over them. Drain well. Slice the cucumber into thin matchsticks.

3 Chop the chilies, garlic, and scallions and put in a liquidizer with the lemon juice, soy sauce, and sugar. Blend thoroughly.

4 Arrange the bean sprouts, cucumber, and fried tofu cubes on a bed of cooked rice. Pour the sauce over and serve immediately.

Gado~gado

THIS IS PROBABLY THE BEST-KNOWN INDONESIAN DISH OF THEM ALL. THERE ARE INNUMERABLE VARIATIONS.

2 cups/1 pound/455g firm tofu

3 tablespoons vegetable oil

1 onion

2–3 cloves garlic

1⅓ cups/10 fl oz/285ml hot water

1 cup/½ pound/225g crunchy peanut butter

2 teaspoons dark brown sugar

½ teaspoon sambal oelek or 1 teaspoon Tabasco sauce

Juice and rind of 1 lemon

1 tablespoon grated fresh ginger

⅔ cup/5 fl oz/140ml coconut milk (or 1–2 oz/30–55g creamed coconut diluted with ¾ cup/7 fl oz/200ml hot water)

½ pound/225g shredded cabbage

½ pound/225g green beans

½ pound/225g fresh bean sprouts

¼ cucumber

1 Cut the tofu into cubes and sauté in 2 tablespoons of the oil until golden brown. Remove from the heat.

2 Chop the onion and garlic finely and fry in the remaining oil until lightly browned.

3 Stir the hot water and peanut butter into the onion and garlic. Stir over a low heat until the peanut butter has melted. Add the sugar, sambal oelek or Tabasco sauce, lemon juice and rind, ginger, and coconut milk, stirring well until thoroughly blended.

4 Blanch the cabbage and green beans in salted boiling water (the bean sprouts may be blanched or served raw). Slice the cucumber. Arrange the vegetables on a plate, top with the tofu cubes and pour the sauce over everything.

Teriyaki Tofu

THIS IS A WESTERNIZED VERSION OF A TRADITIONAL JAPANESE STYLE OF COOKERY. IT COULD BE SERVED WITH RICE AND STIR-FRIED VEGETABLES, OR WESTERN-STYLE WITH A BAKED POTATO AND SALAD OR COOKED SEASONAL VEGETABLES. VEGANS WHO DON'T EAT HONEY COULD SUBSTITUTE RAW CANE SUGAR IN THIS RECIPE.

2 cups/1 pound/455g firm tofu
²/₃ cup/5 fl oz/140ml soy sauce
²/₃ cup/5 fl oz/140ml water
1–2 tablespoons honey
2 teaspoons ground ginger
¹/₂ teaspoon garlic salt
3 teaspoons sesame oil
2 teaspoons mustard
Freshly ground black pepper
 as required

1 Cut the tofu into 8–12 slices and set aside.

2 In a small bowl, combine the soy sauce, water, honey, ginger, garlic salt, sesame oil, and mustard and mix well with a fork. Grind in a little black pepper.

3 Place the tofu slices in a shallow dish and pour the marinade over them. Cover and leave to marinate in the refrigerator for at least an hour, turning once or twice, if possible, during that time.

4 Remove the tofu slices from the marinade and drain them briefly on paper towels. Place the tofu slices under a hot broiler and broil for 3–4 minutes on each side.

Malaysian Noodles

TOFU IS ALSO FOUND IN MALAYSIAN DISHES. THIS IS A RICH, AROMATIC MIXTURE.

2 teaspoons coriander seeds

Seeds from 2 cardamom pods

2 teaspoons cumin seeds

2 teaspoons turmeric

$^1/_2$ teaspoon ground cinnamon

Pinch of ground cloves

2 teaspoons ground fenugreek

4 onions

4 tomatoes

$1^1/_2$–2 cups/$^3/_4$–1 pound/340–455g firm tofu

$^1/_4$ cup/2 oz/55g vegan margarine

3 cloves garlic

2 teaspoons sea salt

2 teaspoons chili powder

1 tablespoon finely chopped fresh ginger

$^2/_3$ cup/5 fl oz/140ml water

Juice of 1 lemon

$^3/_4$ pound/340g flat rice noodles

1–2 tablespoons chopped parsley

1 Heat all the spices in a dry heavy skillet until aromatic, then grind in a mortar or food processor until pulverized.

2 Chop the onions coarsely, then blend in a liquidizer. Peel and chop the tomatoes. Dice the tofu.

3 Melt the margarine in a pan, add the puréed onion and sauté, stirring until lightly browned. Add the tomatoes and fry for 1–2 minutes, then add the diced tofu and stir-fry for 2–3 minutes.

4 Mince the garlic and add to the saucepan, along with the salt, chili powder, ginger, and the spice mixture, stirring well.

5 Add a little of the water and simmer over a low heat for a few minutes. Now stir in the rest of the water and the lemon juice and leave to simmer for about 5 minutes.

6 Boil the rice noodles until just tender and drain.

7 Toss the tofu mixture with the rice noodles and garnish with the parsley.

Korean Kebabs

THIS IS ANOTHER RECIPE FOR KEBABS, IN WHICH THE TOFU IS DEEP FRIED.

1–1½ cups/³/₄–1 pound/340–455g tofu

Oil for deep frying as required

2 scallions

2 cloves garlic

4 tablespoons miso

1 tablespoon raw cane sugar

2 teaspoons sesame oil

1 tablespoon tahini

Few drops Tabasco sauce

²/₃ cup/5 fl oz/140ml water

12 mushrooms

1 green bell pepper

1 small apple

¼ cucumber

4 small tomatoes

4 oz/115g fresh or canned pineapple
    chunks

1 Drain the tofu well. Cut into cubes and deep fry until golden. Drain and set aside.

2 Chop the scallions finely. Mince the garlic.

3 Combine the miso, sugar, sesame oil, tahini, scallions, garlic, and Tabasco sauce in a large bowl and mix well. Add the water and stir until smooth.

4 Remove the stalks from the mushrooms. Cut the bell pepper and apple into bite-sized chunks. Slice the cucumber. Halve the tomatoes.

5 Add the vegetables and fruit to the miso mixture together with the tofu cubes. Mix thoroughly. Leave to marinate for at least an hour, turning occasionally.

6 Thread everything on to skewers and place under a hot broiler. Broil for about 5 minutes on one side, turn over, pour a little of the marinade over everything and broil the other side for about 5 minutes.

7 Serve with the remainder of the marinade poured over as a sauce.

Japanese Tempeh Kebabs

THIS IS A JAPANESE-STYLE MARINADE WHICH WORKS VERY WELL FOR KEBABS.

1½ cups/¾ pound/340g tempeh

4 tablespoons soy sauce

2 tablespoons cider vinegar or wine vinegar

3 tablespoons water

Juice of ½ lemon

2 teaspoons sesame oil

¾ inch/2cm fresh ginger

2 cloves garlic

1 teaspoon mustard powder

½ pound/225g zucchini

2 cups/4 oz/115g mushrooms

6–8 small tomatoes

1. Dice the tempeh into small cubes, then steam it for about a quarter of an hour. Cool the tempeh.
2. In a mixing bowl combine the soy sauce, vinegar, water, lemon juice, and sesame oil.
3. Grate the ginger finely. Mince the garlic. Add to the above mixture, together with the mustard powder. Mix well, then transfer to a shallow dish.
4. After the tempeh has cooled, place the cubes in the marinade and turn well. Cover and leave in the refrigerator for an hour or more to marinate, turning the cubes from time to time.
5. Slice the zucchini. Clean the mushrooms and remove the stalks. Remove stalks, if necessary, from the tomatoes.
6. Thread the tempeh and vegetables alternately on skewers. Place under a hot broiler and broil until well browned, turning from time to time, and pouring any remaining marinade over the cubes.

Italian Classics

Classic food for sharing with friends and family, Italian cuisine is distinctive both for its fine flavors and its nutritional strengths.

The Mediterranean diet is renowned for its age defying, and heart-health promoting qualities. Olive oil, simple pasta, and fresh produce grown in the Italian sunshine provide one of the richest natural sources of omega oils, and antioxidants. Enjoy!

Gnocchi alla Romana

THIS IS A VEGAN ADAPTATION OF A TRADITIONAL ITALIAN DISH. THE SAUCE CAN BE EITHER HOME-MADE OR A GOOD QUALITY SAUCE FROM A STORE. A QUICK RECIPE.

5 cups/40 fl oz/1120ml soy milk
Sea salt as required
Freshly ground black pepper
   as required
Nutmeg as required
2 cups/½ pound/225g whole-wheat
   farina
2 oz/55g nutritional yeast or 2
   tablespoons vegan Parmesan
⅓ cup/3 oz/85g vegan margarine
Tomato sauce as required

1 Heat the milk in a saucepan, seasoning it with salt, pepper, and a good grating of nutmeg. Sprinkle in the farina and bring to a boil. Stir continuously over a low heat until thickened.

2 Stir half the yeast or vegan Parmesan and ¼ cup/2 oz/55g of the margarine into the farina, then spread it on an oiled dish and smooth it down to about ½ inch/1.5cm. Cool and then chill until ready to prepare.

3 Cut the mixture into small squares and put the squares, overlapping if desired, into an oiled shallow ovenproof dish. Sprinkle with the other half of the yeast or vegan Parmesan, and top with small pieces of the remaining margarine.

4 Bake at 400°F/200°C/Gas Mark 6 for about 20 minutes.

5 Serve with tomato sauce.

Risi e Bisi

SMOKED TOFU CAN ADD A NEW DIMENSION TO ITALIAN DISHES.

2 cups/³/₄ pound/340g brown rice

2 teaspoons yeast extract

³/₄ cup/6 oz/170g smoked tofu

2 tablespoons vegan margarine

2 tablespoons olive oil

1 cup/1 oz/30g chopped parsley

2 sticks celery

1 pound/455g fresh (shelled) or frozen peas

4 tablespoons cider vinegar or wine vinegar

Sea salt as required

Freshly ground black pepper as required

3 tablespoons nutritional yeast

1 Put the rice in a pan, cover with boiling water, and add the yeast extract instead of salt. Cook until the rice is tender and the water is absorbed.

2 Cut the smoked tofu into small cubes. Sauté the cubes in the margarine and olive oil for about 5 minutes.

3 Chop the parsley and celery, add them to the smoked tofu and cook for 3–4 minutes. Add the peas and vinegar, stir well, raise the heat for 2–3 minutes, then cover the saucepan, lower the heat and cook for a few minutes until just tender.

4 Stir this mixture into the cooked rice and leave for 1–2 minutes. Finally, stir in the seasoning and the yeast. Serve immediately.

Italian Bread Salad

THIS SALAD PROVIDES A GOOD WAY OF RECYCLING BREAD THAT HAS NOT BEEN EATEN WHILE FRESH.

1 pound/455g stale whole-wheat bread

²/₃ cup/5 fl oz/140ml water

1 clove garlic

1 onion

³/₄ cup/6 oz/200g tomatoes

3 tablespoons vegetable oil

1 tablespoon cider vinegar or wine
  vinegar

Sea salt as required

Freshly ground black pepper as required

2 teaspoons dried basil or 2
  tablespoons fresh basil

1 Dice the bread and soak it in the water for 10 minutes or
  more. Drain off the surplus moisture.

2 Cut the garlic in two and rub the salad bowl with it.

3 Chop the onion finely, and peel and dice the tomatoes.

4 Combine the bread with the onion and tomatoes. Add the oil
  and vinegar with the seasoning and mix lightly together.

5 Sprinkle with basil and serve.

Fettuccine All' Alfredo

MANY ITALIAN RESTAURANTS MAKE A FEATURE OF PASTA WITH A RICH CREAM SAUCE. NOW THAT THERE ARE GOOD, NOT-TOO-SWEET NON-DAIRY CREAMS AVAILABLE, VEGANS CAN ALSO ENJOY SUCH DISHES. A QUICK RECIPE.

12–14 oz/240–395g whole-wheat
  fettuccine

¹/₄ cup/2 oz/55g vegan margarine

1–1¹/₂ cups/2 cartons (120g each)
  vegan cream

¹/₂ cup/2 oz/55g nutritional yeast or 2
  tablespoons vegan Parmesan

Sea salt as required

Freshly ground black pepper as required

1 Cook the fettuccine until just tender then drain.

2 Melt the margarine over a low heat in a large saucepan.
  Lower the heat to minimum, add the cream and gently heat
  it until warm. Alternatively, heat the margarine and cream
  in the microwave until melted and warm.

3 Add the fettuccine to the melted margarine and cream, add a
  little salt and lots of pepper and mix well. Sprinkle yeast or
  vegan Parmesan over the top. Place under a heated broiler
  for a couple of minutes to brown the top, and serve.

Spaghetti with Chestnut Sauce

CHESTNUTS MAKE A DELICIOUS BASIS FOR THIS PASTA SAUCE.

$^1/_2$ pound/225g dried chestnuts soaked in a Thermos flask overnight (see page 104)

2 onions

2 tablespoons extra virgin olive oil

1 pound/455g tomatoes

2 tablespoons water

Sea salt as required

Freshly ground black pepper as required

1 teaspoon dried or 1 tablespoon fresh marjoram

12–14 oz/340–395g whole-wheat spaghetti

1 Drain the chestnuts.

2 Chop the onions. Heat the oil in a saucepan and sauté the onions for a few minutes. Add the chestnuts to the pan and cook 3–4 minutes longer.

3 Peel and chop the tomatoes. Add them to the saucepan together with the water, seasonings, and marjoram. Cover the pan and cook over a very low heat for 10–15 minutes, stirring constantly.

4 Cook the spaghetti until just tender; drain and top with the chestnut sauce.

Lasagne al Forno with Tempeh

TEMPEH MAKES A GOOD FILLING FOR LASAGNE, AND TOFU ADDS LOW-FAT CREAMINESS.

6 oz/170g whole-wheat lasagne

1¹/₂ cups/12 oz/340g tempeh

2 onions

2 cloves garlic

2 tablespoons vegetable oil

2 cups/4 oz/115g mushrooms

2 cans (14–16 oz/400g each) tomatoes

4 tablespoons tomato paste

2 teaspoons oregano

Freshly ground black pepper as
    required

2 cups/1 pound/455g tofu

3 tablespoons tahini

1 tablespoon soy sauce

2 tablespoons soy yogurt

Juice of ¹/₂ lemon

1 Cook the lasagne in boiling water until tender. Drain. (Alternatively, use a precooked variety, in which case it is preferable to make the dish several hours in advance and store in the refrigerator until ready to bake or microwave.)

2 Steam the tempeh in a mixture of 4 parts water to 1 part soy sauce. Cool.

3 Chop the onions. Mince the garlic. Sauté in the oil in a saucepan for 3–4 minutes.

4 Chop the mushrooms finely. Add to the saucepan, together with the tomatoes, paste, and oregano. Bring to a boil, then lower the heat and simmer, uncovered, for about 10 minutes.

5 Crumble the tempeh into the saucepan and continue simmering for about 10 minutes. Season to taste – additional salt should not be required.

6 Meanwhile, put the tofu, tahini, soy sauce, yogurt, and lemon juice in a liquidizer and blend thoroughly.

7 Put alternate layers of lasagne, tempeh, sauce, and blended tofu in a casserole dish, finishing with a layer of tofu. Bake at 350°F/180°C/Gas Mark 4 for about half an hour. Alternatively, cover with wax paper and microwave for 6–7 minutes.

Spinach and Mushroom Lasagne

THIS DISH WOULD BE A GOOD CHOICE FOR ENTERTAINING DINNER GUESTS.

1 pound/455g spinach

¼ cup/2 oz/55g vegan margarine

1 teaspoon dried marjoram

Sea salt as required

Freshly ground black pepper as
    required

1½–2 cups/¾–1 pound/340–455g
    firm tofu

4 cups/½ pound/225g mushrooms

4 tablespoon whole-wheat flour

2 teaspoon soy sauce

8–10 oz/225–285g whole-wheat
    lasagne

1 Wash the spinach well, then cook it in a saucepan without
   additional water until it is just tender. Drain, reserving the
   liquid.

2 Chop the spinach coarsely and, while it is still warm, mix in
   half the margarine. Season with the marjoram, salt and
   pepper, then crumble the tofu into the spinach mixture and
   combine thoroughly.

3 Chop the mushrooms finely. Sauté in the remaining
   margarine until tender. Stir in the flour. Make up the
   spinach liquid with water to 1⅓ cups/10 fl oz/285ml and stir
   it into the mushrooms gradually until it thickens and boils.
   Mix in the soy sauce.

4 Cook the lasagne in salted boiling water until tender, 15–20
   minutes. Drain well.

5 Place alternate layers of lasagne, spinach/tofu mixture, and
   mushroom sauce in an ovenproof dish, finishing with
   mushroom sauce.

6 Bake in the oven at 400°F/200°C/Gas Mark 6 for half
   an hour.

Italian Macaroni and Beans

THIS IS A VEGAN VERSION OF A TRADITIONAL ITALIAN DISH. IT IS PRACTICALLY VEGAN IN ITS NATURAL STATE, BUT THE YEAST OR VEGAN PARMESAN ADDS A LOVELY FLAVOR. SERVE IT WITH A GREEN SALAD. A QUICK RECIPE.

3 cups/$^3/_4$ pound/340g whole-wheat macaroni

2$^1/_2$ cups/1 pound/455g or 2 cans (14–16 oz/400g each) cooked drained garbanzo beans

4 tablespoons extra virgin olive oil

2–3 cloves garlic

Freshly ground black pepper as required

Nutritional yeast or vegan Parmesan as required

1 Cook the macaroni until just tender, then drain. Drain the garbanzo beans.

2 Heat the oil in a saucepan. Mince the garlic and add it to the pan, stirring for a minute or two. Add the garbanzo beans and macaroni, and continue stirring. Season with pepper (if the beans and pasta were cooked in salted water additional salt should not be needed).

3 Spoon the mixture into serving dishes and sprinkle with lots of yeast or vegan Parmesan.

Potato Gnocchi

USE A HOME-MADE TOMATO SAUCE OR A GOOD QUALITY BOTTLED VARIETY FOR THIS CLASSIC ITALIAN POTATO DISH.

3 pounds/1350g potatoes

2 cups/$^1/_2$ pound/225g whole-wheat
  flour

$^1/_4$ cup/2 oz/55g vegan margarine

8 tablespoons water

8 tablespoons chick pea flour

Sea salt as required

Freshly ground black pepper
  as required

Tomato sauce as required

Nutritional yeast or vegan Parmesan
  as required

1 Cook the potatoes. Drain them and place them back in the pan and over the heat again. Shake them around the pan so that they are well dried out. Remove the skins and mash the potatoes in a large bowl.

2 Add the flour and margarine to the potatoes. Stir the chick pea flour into the water with a fork and add this to the potatoes. Mix well and season to taste. (This can all be done well in advance and the mixture left in the refrigerator until meal time.)

3 Heat the water to boiling point in a large saucepan and sprinkle in a little sea salt. Tear off walnut-sized balls from the potato mixture and drop them into the water. (This will probably have to be done in three or four stages.) When the water has returned to a boil, lower the heat and simmer the gnocchi for a few minutes. (They will rise to the surface.) Either remove them individually with a slotted spoon or carefully drain the pan into a colander.

4 Serve the gnocchi topped with a well-flavored tomato sauce and sprinkled with nutritional yeast if desired or vegan Parmesan.

Risotto

COMPLETE DISHES LIKE THIS ONE ARE ALWAYS USEFUL BECAUSE THERE IS NO NEED TO WORRY ABOUT VEGETABLE ACCOMPANIMENTS.

2 cups/³/₄ pound/340g brown rice

2 small onions

¹/₃ cup/3 oz/85g vegan margarine

Vegetable bouillon or water as
    required

1 stick celery

1 green bell pepper

1 cup/2 oz/55g mushrooms

1 clove garlic

1¹/₄–1¹/₂ cups/10–12 oz/285–340g firm
    tofu

2 tablespoons cider vinegar or wine
    vinegar

¹/₃ cup/2 oz/55g soy bakon bits

¹/₂ teaspoon dried basil

¹/₂ teaspoon dried marjoram

1   Cover the rice with boiling water, leave to soak for several hours, then drain.

2   Chop 1 onion. Melt half the margarine in a pan and sauté the onion until tender. Add the rice, cover with vegetable bouillon or water, bring to a boil, then simmer.

3   Meanwhile, chop the remaining onion, the celery, bell pepper, and mushrooms. Mince the garlic and dice the tofu. Melt the remaining margarine in a separate pan and sauté the vegetables and tofu for a few minutes until tender. Add the vinegar, soy bakon bits, and herbs. Cover and simmer for about 5 minutes.

4   When the rice is nearly ready add the vegetable and tofu mixture to it, stirring well, and continue cooking until the liquid is completely absorbed.

Cacciatore

1 small onion

1 carrot

1 clove garlic

4 tablespoons vegetable oil

1 bay leaf

²/₃ cup/5 oz/140g tomato paste

1¹/₂ cups/12 fl oz/340ml water

2–3 cups/¹/₂–³/₄ pound/225–340g
   whole-wheat macaroni or pasta
   shells

2 cups/1 pound/455g firm tofu

¹/₄–¹/₂ cup/1–2 oz/30–55g whole-wheat
   flour

1 teaspoon dried basil

²/₃ cup/4 oz/115g fresh (shelled) or
   frozen peas

1 Chop the onion, carrot, and garlic and sauté in half the oil,
   along with the bay leaf, for a few minutes. Add the tomato
   paste and water, bring to a boil and simmer for about
   10 minutes.

2 Meanwhile, cook the macaroni for 10–15 minutes in salted
   boiling water.

3 Cut the tofu into cubes. Dust lightly with the flour and basil
   and sauté in the remaining oil until lightly browned.

4 Add the tofu to the tomato sauce, along with the peas, and
   simmer until the peas are just tender.

5 Serve with the cooked macaroni.

Tofu Italian Pizza

IN ITALY CHEESE IS BY NO MEANS CONSIDERED AN ESSENTIAL INGREDIENT IN A PIZZA: A WELL-FLAVORED TOMATO SAUCE IS THE KEY COMPONENT. HOWEVER, AN ALL-VEGETABLE TOPPING MEANS A LOW-PROTEIN DISH, WHEREAS BY INCLUDING TOFU YOU GET A NEW TASTE AND TEXTURE PLUS PROTEIN.

DOUGH

1 teaspoon raw cane sugar

²/₃ cup/5 fl oz/140ml water at blood heat (a little more if required)

1 teaspoon dried yeast

2 cups/½ pound/225g whole-wheat flour

1 teaspoon sea salt

TOPPING

1 onion

2 cloves garlic

2 tablespoons olive oil

1 can (14–16 oz/400g) tomatoes

2 tablespoons tomato paste

2 teaspoons dried oregano

1 teaspoon dried basil

Sea salt as required

Freshly ground black pepper as required

1–1½ cups/½–¾ pound/225–340g firm or medium tofu

1–2 cups/2–4 oz/55–115g mushrooms

1 small green bell pepper

OPTIONAL EXTRAS

Sliced olives, capers, onions, artichoke hearts as required

1 Dissolve the sugar in half the water, then sprinkle in the yeast and mix with a fork. Cover and leave in a warm place for about 10 minutes, by which time it should be frothy. Put the flour and salt in a bowl, then pour in the yeast mixture, along with the remaining water. Add a little extra water if necessary to make a moist dough. Knead for 5 minutes. Roll out the dough and use to line pizza pans. Cover and leave in a warm place for about half an hour.

2 Chop the onion and garlic and sauté in the olive oil until tender. Add the tomatoes, tomato paste, and herbs, bring to a boil then simmer until thick – about half an hour. Season to taste.

3 Spread the sauce over the pizza base – you can make one large pizza or two small ones. (Any leftover sauce can be refrigerated for use within a week.) Crumble the tofu over the sauce.

4 Chop the mushrooms finely; thinly slice the bell pepper. Arrange over the tofu along with any of the optional extras.

5 Bake in the oven at 450°F/230°C/Gas Mark 8 for about half an hour.

Calzone

TRADITIONALLY CALZONE IS MADE WITH A YEAST DOUGH AS IN THE TWO PREVIOUS RECIPES, BUT A SHORTCRUST PASTRY WORKS WELL.

1 onion

1–2 cloves garlic

2 tablespoons olive oil

1 carrot

2 sticks celery

1 small green bell pepper

1 cup/2 oz/55g mushrooms

4 tablespoons tomato paste

$^1/_3$ cup/3 fl oz/90ml water

1 teaspoon dried basil

1 teaspoon dried oregano

1 cup/$^1/_2$ pound/225g firm or
   medium tofu

2 cups/$^1/_2$ pound/225g whole-wheat
   flour

Sea salt as required

$^1/_2$ cup/4 oz/115g vegan margarine

1 Chop the onion and garlic and sauté in the olive oil for 3–4 minutes.

2 Chop the carrot, celery, and bell pepper and add to the pan. Chop the mushrooms and add to the pan when the other vegetables are nearly tender. Stir in the tomato paste, water, basil, and oregano and bring to a boil. Cut the tofu into cubes and add to the pan. Lower the heat and simmer for 5 minutes. Cool slightly.

3 Put the flour and salt in a bowl and mix in the margarine. Add enough water to make a dough, divide into 4 pieces, and roll out into circles on a floured board.

4 Spoon a quarter of the filling on to half of each circle. Fold the dough over to cover, and pinch it well to seal.

5 Bake in the oven at 375°F/190°C/Gas Mark 5 for 25–35 minutes until the crust is browned.

Eggplant Parmigiana

SERVE THIS DISH ON ITS OWN OR WITH SALAD FOR A LIGHT LUNCH, OR WITH POTATOES OR RICE FOR A MORE SUBSTANTIAL MEAL.

1 can (14–16 oz/400g) tomatoes

1 onion

2 cloves garlic

3 teaspoons dried basil

1 tablespoon vegetable oil plus
    additional as required

1–1½ pound/455–680g eggplants

Fine bread crumbs or whole-wheat
    flour as required

1½–2 cups/¾–1 pound/340–455g
    firm tofu

1 Blend the tomatoes in a liquidizer then pour into a saucepan. Chop the onion and mince the garlic, add to the saucepan along with the basil and the 1 tablespoon vegetable oil. Stir well, bring to a boil, then lower the heat and simmer for about 20 minutes.

2 Slice the eggplants very thinly. Brush each slice with a little oil on both sides, then dip into fine bread crumbs or flour. Put the slices under the broiler and broil until tender, turning them over once. (Alternatively, shallow-fry the slices in a little oil and drain well.)

3 Arrange half the eggplant slices in an oiled baking dish, crumble half the tofu over them, top with half the tomato sauce. Repeat the layers.

4 Bake in the oven at 350°F/180°C/Gas Mark 4 for 20–30 minutes.

Fettuccine with Creamy Tofu Sauce

THIS IS AMAZINGLY QUICK AND EASY. A CRISP GREEN SALAD WOULD PROVIDE A GOOD CONTRAST OF TEXTURE AND FLAVOR.

1½ cups/¾ pound/340g medium tofu
⅔ cup/5 fl oz/140ml soy yogurt
1 tablespoon tahini
2 heaped teaspoons miso
1 tablespoon lemon juice
2½ cups/12–14 oz/340–400g
    whole-wheat fettuccine
Freshly ground black pepper
    as required

1 Put the tofu, yogurt, tahini, miso, and lemon juice in a liquidizer and blend well.
2 Cook the pasta in salted boiling water until just tender, then drain.
3 Toss the tagliatelle with the tofu sauce, grind some black pepper over the top and serve at once.

Ravioli

FOR CONVENIENCE, SERVE THIS DISH WITH ONE OF THE NATURAL TOMATO SAUCES AVAILABLE AT HEALTH-FOOD STORES.

3 cups/³/₄ pound/340g wholemeal or
   84% flour
2 tablespoons soy flour
Pinch of sea salt
²/₃ cup/5 fl oz/140ml warm water
1 cup/¹/₂ pound/225g firm tofu
¹/₂ teaspoon onion salt
¹/₂ teaspoon garlic salt
Freshly ground black pepper
   as required

1 Mix the flour, soy flour, and salt together in a bowl and add the water to make a dough (do this slowly as different flours require slightly different quantities of liquid and once the consistency of a dough has been reached no more water should be added). Knead well and set aside.

2 Mash the tofu in a mixing bowl. Stir in the onion and garlic salts and a little black pepper.

3 Divide the dough into 4 or more sections and roll out on a floured board. Cut out small squares. Place a little filling on to a square, cover with another square, and seal all round the edges with a fork to secure the filling inside.

4 Drop the squares into a large pan of salted boiling water and cook for 10 minutes. Drain well, and serve with tomato sauce.

Spaghetti Milanese

ANOTHER COMPLETE DISH UTILIZING SMOKED TOFU, AND ANOTHER ONE THAT'S EASY TO MAKE.

$^3/_4$ pound/340g whole-wheat spaghetti

1 onion

2 cups/4 oz/115g mushrooms

3 tablespoons vegan margarine

Grating nutmeg

Pinch of dried thyme

Freshly ground black pepper
  as required

1 can (14–16 oz/400g) tomatoes

1 cup/$^1/_2$ pound/225g smoked tofu

Nutritional yeast as required

1 Cook the spaghetti in salted boiling water until tender.

2 Meanwhile, chop the onion and mushrooms and cook in 2 tablespoons of the margarine for 3–5 minutes.

3 Add the nutmeg, thyme, black pepper, and tomatoes and stir well. Bring to a boil, lower the heat and simmer for about 15 minutes.

4 Chop the smoked tofu into small dice and add to the saucepan. Cook for 5 minutes.

5 Drain the spaghetti and toss with the remaining margarine.

6 Serve the spaghetti with the sauce poured over it, sprinkled with yeast.

American Classics

It's probably true to say that many of the classic American dishes are high in saturated fats and added salt and sugar — so when we want to choose a healthy option our favorites are often high on the list of no no's.

Not so with this collection though — which includes pizza and specially created cheeseburgers which adults and children alike will enjoy.

Sausage Bake

THIS DISH IS SIMILAR TO THE TRADITIONAL BRITISH RECIPE TOAD IN THE HOLE.

1¼ cups/5 oz/150g whole-wheat flour

1 cup/4 oz/115g cornmeal

½ teaspoon raw cane sugar

Pinch of sea salt

2 teaspoons baking powder

1 teaspoon baking soda

4 tablespoons vegetable oil

1⅓–2 cups/10–15 fl oz/285–425ml soy yogurt

1–1½ pounds/455–680g vegan sausages

1 Put the dry ingredients in a bowl and mix. Add the oil. Add enough water to the yogurt to make it up to 2½ cups/20 fl oz/570ml, and add it to the bowl. Mix with a large spoon.

2 Put the sausages into an oiled casserole dish and cover with the batter. Bake at 425°F/220°C/Gas Mark 7 for 20–25 minutes until lightly browned and set.

Stuffed Pancakes

THIS IS SIMPLE AND DELICIOUS. SERVE THE PANCAKES WITH A GREEN SALAD.

Crêpe batter (see page 288)

14–16 oz/340–455g vegetable pâté

1 tablespoon soy milk

4 large tomatoes

Vegan margarine or vegetable oil for frying as required

1 Beat the pâté with the milk.

2 Chop the tomatoes roughly.

3 Heat the margarine or oil, pour in a little batter at a time and fry on both sides.

4 Fill each pancake with a little pâté and some of the chopped tomato.

Nutmeat Hash

THIS IS A MEAT-FREE VERSION OF A TRULY AMERICAN DISH.

2 onions

2 tablespoons vegetable oil

2 teaspoons yeast extract

2 small or 1 large can (1$^{1}/_{4}$–1$^{1}/_{2}$
   pounds/565–680g) nut savory

1$^{1}/_{2}$ pounds/680g potatoes

1 green bell pepper

1 clove garlic

1$^{1}/_{3}$ cups/10 fl oz/285ml vegetable
   bouillon

Sea salt as required

Freshly ground black pepper
   as required

1 Chop the onions. Sauté them in the oil until tenderized. Add
   the yeast extract.

2 Mash the nutmeat. Grate the potatoes coarsely. Chop the
   bell pepper finely. Mince the garlic. Combine those
   ingredients with the onion and stir in the bouillon. Season
   to taste.

3 Turn the mixture on to an oiled baking sheet and pat it
   down to a thickness of $^{3}/_{4}$–1 inch. Cover the top with foil.

4 Bake at 350°F/180°C/Gas Mark 4 for about 15 minutes,
   then lower the heat to 300°F/160°C/Gas Mark 2 and cook
   for another half hour.

Tempeh Hash with Potatoes

"HASH" IS AN ALL-AMERICAN FAVORITE — THIS IS A MEAT-FREE ADAPTATION OF THE ORIGINAL RECIPE.

2 cups/1 pound/455g potatoes

2¹/₂ cups/20 fl oz/570ml water

4 teaspoons yeast extract

1 pound/455g tempeh

1 onion

1 green bell pepper

4 tablespoons vegetable oil

2 tablespoons whole-wheat flour

2 tablespoons tomato paste

Freshly ground black pepper
    as required

1 Cook the potatoes.

2 Heat 1¹/₃ cups/10 fl oz/285ml water and dissolve 2 teaspoons yeast extract in it. Place the tempeh in the saucepan, lower the heat and simmer for 5–7 minutes before turning over and simmering for 5–7 minutes on the other side. The liquid should have mostly been absorbed by now but if there is any left, drain it. Chop the tempeh finely and set aside. (If desired, steps 1–2 can be carried out in advance, and the tempeh and potato kept refrigerated until ready to prepare the dish.)

3 Chop the onion and bell pepper finely. Fry in the oil for 3–4 minutes until they begin to brown.

4 Dice the tempeh and potato and add them to the saucepan. Cook for a minute or two, stirring constantly. Add the flour and stir well, then slowly pour in the remaining water, stirring constantly. Stir in the remaining yeast extract, the tomato paste, and pepper. Heat thoroughly and serve.

Pecan Roast

THIS IS A NICE SUBSTANTIAL ROAST. SERVE IT WITH SEASONAL VEGETABLES AND POTATOES.

1 small onion
1 cup/6 oz/170g pecans
3 cups/6 oz/170g whole-wheat
   bread crumbs
2 tablespoons minced parsley
5 oz/140g tomato paste
1 cup/8 fl oz/225ml water
Sea salt as required
Freshly ground black pepper
   as required

1 Grate the onion. Chop the nuts.
2 Combine all the ingredients in a large mixing bowl and mix well. Transfer to a baking dish, and bake at 375°F/190°C/Gas Mark 5 for about 40 minutes.

Tomato and Corn Savory

THIS SIMPLE DISH IS ALWAYS APPRECIATED. SERVE OVER BROWN RICE. A QUICK RECIPE.

1 onion
1 small green bell pepper
2 tablespoons vegetable oil
4 large tomatoes
1 can (14–16 oz/400g) corn
2 tablespoons cornstarch
1$^{1}/_{3}$ cups/10 fl oz/285ml water
1 teaspoon garlic salt
3 tablespoons soy bakon bits

1 Chop the onion and bell pepper finely.
2 Sauté them in the vegetable oil until they begin to soften.
3 Chop the tomatoes and add them to the saucepan. Add the corn and sauté for a few more minutes, stirring well.
4 Dissolve the cornstarch in a little water, add the rest of the water, mix well and add to the saucepan. Bring to a boil, stirring constantly.
5 Add the garlic salt and soy bakon bits and simmer for a few more minutes.

Eggplants Creole-Style

THIS EGGPLANT DISH IS BEST ACCOMPANIED BY BOILED OR BAKED POTATOES.

1–1½ pound/455–680g eggplants

⅓ cup/3 oz/85g vegan margarine

½ cup/2 oz/55g whole-wheat flour

1½ pound/680g ripe tomatoes

2 small green bell peppers

2 small onions

1 teaspoon sea salt

2 teaspoons raw cane sugar

1 bay leaf

3 cloves

1 cup/2 oz/55g whole-wheat
   bread crumbs

1 Peel and dice the eggplants. Cook for 10 minutes in boiling water then drain well and place in an oiled baking dish.

2 Melt ¼ cup/2 oz/55g of the margarine and stir in the flour.

3 Peel and slice the tomatoes, chop the bell peppers and onions and add these to the saucepan, stirring well.

4 Add the salt, sugar, bay leaf, and cloves and cook for 5 minutes.

5 Pour the mixture over the eggplants. Cover with the bread crumbs and top with the rest of the margarine.

6 Bake in a moderate oven at 350°F/180°C/Gas Mark 4 for about half an hour. Alternatively, cover with wax paper and microwave for 6–7 minutes.

Kidney Bean Cheeseburgers

SERVE THESE BURGERS IN A BUN WITH THE USUAL BURGER TRIMMING. A QUICK RECIPE.

2½ cups/1 pound/455g or 2 cans
   (14–16 oz/400g each) cooked
   drained kidney beans

½ cup/2 oz/55g rolled oats

2 tablespoons soy sauce

2 tablespoons vegetable oil

vegan cheese slices to serve

1 Drain and mash the beans in a bowl (a potato masher or pastry blender is useful for this).

2 Add the oats and soy sauce and knead well with the hands. Form into four large burgers.

3 Sauté them in the oil on each side, starting out with a high heat to brown, then lowering the heat so that they are cooked right through.

4 Serve in a bun, topped with a slice of dairy-free cheese.

Virginian Black-eyed Beans

THIS IS AN UNUSUAL AND DELICIOUS COMBINATION OF INGREDIENTS WHICH BENEFITS GREATLY FROM BEING SERVED WITH CORNBREAD.

1¹/₂ cups/³/₄ pound/340g black-eyed
   beans
1 onion
1 bay leaf
¹/₂ teaspoon thyme
3 whole cloves
Sea salt as required
Freshly ground black pepper
   as required

1 Cover the beans with boiling water, leave to soak for several hours or overnight, then drain.
2 Chop the onion coarsely and combine it with the beans in a saucepan. Cover with water and add the bay leaf, thyme, and cloves.
3 Cook over a low heat until the beans are tender – about 45 minutes. If necessary, add additional water to prevent drying out. Season to taste.
4 Serve with Southern Cornbread (see below).

Southern Cornbread

1 cup/4 oz/115g whole-wheat flour
³/₄ cup/4 oz/115g cornmeal
2 tablespoons raw cane sugar
4 teaspoons baking powder
1 teaspoon sea salt
³/₄ cup/7 fl oz/200ml soy milk
¹/₃ cup/3 oz/85g vegan margarine

1 Mix the flour, cornmeal, sugar, baking powder, and salt in a bowl.
2 Melt the margarine and add it, with the milk, to the dry mixture. Stir just until this is moistened, then immediately pour the batter into an oiled baking pan.
3 Bake in a hot oven at 425°/220°C/Gas Mark 7 for about an hour, until the top is golden and firm and drawing away from the edges of the pan.

Quick and Easy Pizza

A TRADITIONAL PIZZA DOUGH IS MADE WITH YEAST, WHICH OF COURSE REQUIRES TIME TO RISE AND TIME TO BAKE, WHEREAS THIS REQUIRES NEITHER. THE TOPPING IS RICH AND FULL OF FLAVOR. SERVE WITH A GREEN SALAD. A QUICK RECIPE.

1³/₄ cups/7 oz/200g whole-wheat flour
5 tablespoons vegetable oil
Pinch of sea salt
2 teaspoons baking powder
1 onion
2 tablespoons tomato paste
5 tablespoons water
2 teaspoons dried oregano
6 black olives
1 tablespoon tahini
1 tablespoon miso

1 Mix the flour with 1 tablespoon oil, the salt, and baking powder, then add sufficient water to make a soft dough. Roll out into two 7 inch/17cm circles for the bases.

2 Chop the onion finely. Fry in 2 tablespoons oil until tender.

3 Mix the tomato paste, 2 tablespoons water, oregano, and the onion in a small bowl.

4 Chop the olives finely.

5 Mix the tahini, miso, and remaining 3 tablespoons water in a small bowl.

6 Heat 1 tablespoon oil in a large skillet. Fry one of the bases for 4–5 minutes, then turn over. Spread with half the tomato mixture, sprinkle with half the olives, and top with half the tahini mixture. Cook for another 4–5 minutes, then place under a medium broiler until the tahini is browned.

7 Repeat with the second base. Serve with a green salad.

American-style Mexican Rice

THIS STYLE OF PREPARING RICE IS CALLED "MEXICAN" EVEN THOUGH THE RICE IN MEXICAN RESTAURANTS IS NOT AT ALL LIKE THIS. THE SOY BAKON BITS GIVE IT EXTRA FLAVOR AND CRUNCH.

$1\frac{1}{4}$ cups/$\frac{1}{2}$ pound/225g brown rice

2 tablespoons vegan margarine

2 onions

1 green bell pepper

2 sticks celery

1 can (14 oz/400g) tomatoes

1 tablespoon tomato paste

2 teaspoons paprika

2 bay leaves

Sea salt as required

Freshly ground black pepper
    as required

$\frac{2}{3}$ cup/5 fl oz/140ml water

2 tablespoons soy bakon bits

1 Cover the rice with boiling water and soak for several hours. Drain well.

2 Slice the onions thinly and sauté in the margarine for 2–3 minutes.

3 Chop the bell pepper and celery and add it to the saucepan. Continue to sauté for 2–3 minutes.

4 Add the rice and stir well. Add the tomatoes, paste, paprika, bay leaves, and seasoning. Stir well. Add the water and bring to a boil. Lower the heat and leave to simmer until the liquid is absorbed and the rice is tender, about 25–30 minutes.

5 Just before serving, remove the bay leaves and stir in the soy bakon bits.

Desserts

Cakes, cookies, pastries, and desserts are the foods we look forward to — the treats that we give ourselves as a booster or at the end of a hard day. Traditionally packed with ingredients such as eggs, butter, milk, and cream, dairy-free dessert dishes need a creative approach and have not always been a jewel in the crown of vegan recipe collections.

This collection should reassure you that there is room for delicious desserts without dairy produce. Including rich desserts and chocolate-based dishes as well a selection of sugar-free and fresh-fruit recipes, these desserts will keep you healthy, and happy.

Cakes & Cookies

Chocolate cake with iced topping is a delight for special occasions – but the cookies in this collection are full of enough goodness to make the perfect snacks and fillers for any day.

Strawberry Shortcake

2 cups/¹/₂ pound/225g whole-wheat
  flour
4 teaspoons baking powder
1 teaspoon sea salt
1 tablespoon raw cane sugar
2 tablespoons–¹/₄ cup/1–2 oz/30–55g
  vegan margarine
²/₃ cup/5 fl oz/140ml soy milk
Fresh strawberries as required

MOCK CREAM
1–2 tablespoons cornstarch
1¹/₃ cups/10 fl oz/285ml soy milk
2 tablespoons–¹/₄ cup/1–2 oz/30–55g
  vegan margarine

1 Mix the flour with the baking powder, salt, and sugar.
2 Add the margarine, cut into small pieces with a pastry
   blender, two knives, or your fingers, and mix until
   thoroughly blended. (The larger amount of margarine will
   make a richer dessert.)
3 Make a well in the center and pour in the milk. Stir in
   vigorously for the shortest possible time then turn the
   dough out on to a floured board.
4 Cut the dough in half and roll out each half. Bake in two
   round cake pans in a hot oven at 425°F/220°C/Gas Mark 7
   for 12–15 minutes.
5 Meanwhile, make the mock cream. Blend the cornstarch to a
   smooth mixture with a little of the milk, then add the rest of
   the milk; pour the mixture into a saucepan and bring slowly
   to the boil, stirring constantly. Cook until thickened, then
   remove from the heat and set aside to cool.
6 Cream the margarine until very soft, but on no account
   warm the margarine. Gradually beat in spoonfuls of the
   cornflour mixture – the more you beat this, the better the
   cream becomes.
7 Allow the cakes to cool, then sandwich and top the layers
   with the cream and strawberries (sweetened if desired).

Plain Sponge Cake

THIS CAN EITHER BE SANDWICHED WITH PRESERVES AND SPRINKLED WITH SUGAR, OR SANDWICHED WITH A "BUTTER" FILLING MADE FROM VEGAN MARGARINE AND CONFECTIONER'S SUGAR OR FINELY GROUND RAW CANE SUGAR AND ICED WITH CARAMEL ICING (SEE BELOW).

¼ cup/2 oz/55g vegan margarine

⅓ cup/2 oz/55g raw cane sugar

1 tablespoon soy flour

2 tablespoons water

Few drops vanilla extract

¾ cup/3½ oz/100g plus 1 tablespoon
   wholewheat self-rising flour

½ teaspoon baking powder

1 tablespoon/½ oz/15g cornstarch

3–4 tablespoons soy milk

1 Beat the margarine and sugar together until fluffy.

2 Mix the soy flour into the water with a fork. Mix it into the margarine mixture, a little at a time. Add the vanilla extract.

3 Mix the flour, baking powder, and cornstarch together. Add them to the bowl, together with enough milk to make a batter of dropping consistency.

4 Put the batter into two 7 inch/18cm cake pans and bake at 375°F/190°C/Gas Mark 5 for about 20 minutes, until it is firm to the touch and beginning to shrink away from the pan.

Caramel Icing

⅚ cup/5 oz/140g raw cane sugar

4 tablespoons soy milk

¼ cup/2 oz/55g vegan margarine

½ teaspoon vanilla extract

1 Mix the sugar, milk, and margarine in a saucepan.

2 Bring to a boil, stirring constantly. Boil for 2–3 minutes.

3 Remove from the heat and beat until lukewarm.

4 Add the vanilla extract and beat to a spreading consistency.

Totally Dairy-Free Christmas Cake

THIS CAKE IS BEST MADE SEVERAL WEEKS BEFORE REQUIRED AND KEPT, WELL WRAPPED, IN A COOL PLACE. TOP WITH MARZIPAN MADE FROM A MIXTURE OF GROUND ALMONDS, SOY FLOUR, LEMON JUICE, AND ALMOND EXTRACT; AND ICE WITH A WHITE GLACÉ ICING.

$^1/_3$ cup/3 oz/85g soft vegetable fat

$^2/_3$ cup/4 oz/115g raw cane sugar

Juice of 2 small oranges

1 cup/4 oz/115g whole-wheat flour

1 tablespoon mixed spice

3 cups/1 pound/455g mixed dried fruit

1 Beat the fat and sugar together.

2 Add the rest of the ingredients and mix thoroughly.

3 Bake in a cake pan lined with oiled wax paper for 3 hours in a slow oven at 300°F/150°C/Gas Mark 2.

4 Allow to cool completely before serving.

Orange Cake

THIS CAKE TASTES GOOD SANDWICHED WITH MARGARINE THAT HAS BEEN MIXED WITH RAW CANE SUGAR AND PURE ORANGE JUICE. AN ORANGE-FLAVORED GLACÉ ICING MAKES A GOOD TOPPING.

$1^3/_4$ cups/7 oz/200g whole-wheat flour

$^2/_3$ cup/4 oz/115g raw cane sugar

$^1/_2$ teaspoon sea salt

1 teaspoon baking soda

4 tablespoons vegetable oil

2 tablespoons pure orange juice

Grated rind of 1 small orange

$^3/_4$ cup/7 fl oz/200ml water

1 In a large bowl mix together thoroughly the flour, sugar, salt, and baking soda.

2 Add the oil, juice, rind, and water. Mix with a fork until all the dry ingredients are moist. Do not beat.

3 Pour the mixture into two oiled (and, if desired, wax-paper-lined) cake pans.

4 Bake in a moderate oven at 350°F/180°C/Gas Mark 4 for 30 minutes, or until the top of the cake springs up when lightly pressed. Leave to cool thoroughly.

Stuffed Pancakes
(p.230)

Hot Cakes served with
maple syrup (p.287)

Strawberry Shortcake (p.244)

Chocolate Cake with
Chocolate Icing (p.247)

Chocolate Cake

2/3 cup/4 oz/115g raw cane sugar

4 teaspoons cocoa or carob powder

1/2 teaspoon sea salt

1 1/2 cups/6 oz/170g whole-wheat flour

3/4 teaspoon baking soda

1/3 cup/3 fl oz/90ml vegetable oil

1 teaspoon vanilla extract

2 teaspoons cider vinegar or wine vinegar

3/4 cup/7 fl oz/200ml cold water

1 Mix thoroughly the sugar, cocoa or carob, salt, flour, and baking soda in a mixing bowl.

2 Add the oil, vanilla extract, and vinegar and pour cold water over the mixture.

3 Combine well with a fork, but do not beat.

4 Pour into two oiled cake pans (lined if desired) and bake in a moderate oven at 350°F/180°C/Gas Mark 4 for 30 minutes or until the cake springs back when lightly pressed. Leave to cool thoroughly.

Chocolate Icing

1/4 cup/2 oz/55g vegan margarine

1/4 cup/1 oz/30g cocoa or carob powder

4 tablespoons soy milk

5/6 cup/5 oz/140g raw cane sugar

1 teaspoon vanilla extract

1 Combine the first four ingredients in a saucepan and bring them to a boil slowly, stirring constantly.

2 Boil for 1 minute.

3 Remove from the heat and beat until cold. Add the vanilla extract and spread the icing on the cake.

Gingerbread

GINGERBREAD CAN REFER TO ANYTHING FROM A LOAF-TYPE CAKE TO A COOKIE. THIS IS SORT OF IN-BETWEEN, BAKED FLAT BUT WITH A CAKE-LIKE TEXTURE. IT HAS A TENDENCY TO FALL APART BUT TASTES GOOD NEVERTHELESS.

$1^{1}/_{2}$ cups/6 oz/170g whole-wheat flour

$^{1}/_{2}$ cup/3 oz/85g raw cane sugar

1 teaspoon baking powder

1 teaspoon baking soda

1 teaspoon ground ginger

$^{1}/_{2}$ teaspoon ground cinnamon

$^{1}/_{2}$ teaspoon nutmeg

Pinch of sea salt

$^{1}/_{4}$ cup/2 oz/55g vegan margarine

$^{1}/_{2}$ cup/6 oz/170g molasses, corn syrup, or a mixture

4 tablespoons water

1 Mix all the dry ingredients together.

2 In a large saucepan gently heat the margarine, molasses/syrup, and water until it has all melted. Remove from the heat and stir in the dry ingredients.

3 Turn the mixture into a square or rectangular baking pan and bake at 375°F/190°C/Gas Mark 5 for 20–30 minutes.

Peanut Butter Oaties

MAKING COOKIES CAN BE FIDDLY, BUT WITH THE "BAR" KIND THERE IS NO NEED TO SHAPE THEM
BEFORE BAKING.

1/4 cup/2 oz/55g vegan margarine
1/4 cup/2 oz/55g peanut butter
Pinch of sea salt
1/2 teaspoon vanilla extract
1/3 cup/2 oz/55g raw cane sugar
1/2 cup/2 oz/30g whole-wheat flour
1/2 cup/2 oz/55g rolled oats
1/4 teaspoon baking soda
2 tablespoons water

1 Put the margarine and peanut butter in a mixing bowl and beat well. Add the salt, vanilla extract, and sugar and beat until light.
2 Add the flour, oats, baking soda, and water to the bowl. Mix thoroughly and turn out into an oiled baking pan, pressing down to 1/4–1/2 inch.
3 Bake for 15–20 minutes at 375°F/190°C/Gas Mark 5. Remove from oven and let cool before slicing into bars.

Cherry Coconut Refrigerator Cookies

¼ cup/2 oz/55g vegan margarine
¼ cup/1½ oz/45g raw cane sugar
1 cup/4 oz/115g whole-wheat flour
Pinch of sea salt
½ teaspoon baking powder
¼ cup/2 fl oz/60ml soy milk
¼ cup/1½ oz/45g shredded coconut
¼ cup/2 oz/55g glace/dried cherries

1 Beat the margarine and sugar in a bowl until light. Mix together the flour, salt, and baking powder. Add the milk to the margarine mixture, then the flour mixture, and finally the coconut and cherries. Mix well, then knead into a dough.

2 Form the mixture into a large roll (like an oversized sausage) and cover with plastic wrap or aluminum foil. Put the roll into the refrigerator and chill thoroughly.

3 When ready to bake, remove the roll from the refrigerator, and slice it into ¼ inch rounds. Place the rounds on an oiled baking sheet, and bake for about 10 minutes at 325°F/170°C/Gas Mark 3.

Chocolate Oat Treats

A QUICK RECIPE.

¾ cup/4 oz/115g raw cane sugar
¼ cup/2 oz/55g vegan margarine
¼ cup/2 fl oz/60ml soy milk
¼ cup/1 oz/30g cocoa or carob powder
¼ cup/1 oz/30g nuts
2 tablespoons/1 oz/30g raisins
1½ cups/6 oz/170g rolled oats
Few drops vanilla extract

1 Mix the sugar, margarine, milk, and cocoa in a pan. Bring to a boil over a medium heat, stirring frequently, then lower the heat to minimum and leave it to boil for 3 minutes.

2 Chop the nuts or use ready-chopped nuts. Chop the raisins if desired.

3 Remove the pan from the heat and stir in the oats, nuts, raisins, and vanilla extract. Drop by spoonfuls on to an oiled baking sheet or plate to form walnut-sized balls – about 20–25. Leave to cool. (If it is a warm day then store them in the refrigerator.)

Sandwiched Cookies

¾ cup/3 oz/85g whole-wheat self-
rising flour

¾ cup/3 oz/85g rolled oats

¾ cup/4 oz/115g raw cane sugar

⅓ cup/3 oz/85g vegan margarine

½ cup/6 oz/170g raw sugar or sugar-
free preserves

1 Put the dry ingredients in a mixing bowl. Rub in the
margarine until the mixture is crumbly.

2 Place half the mixture in the bottom of an oiled baking pan.
Spread with preserves. Cover with the remaining mixture.

3 Bake at 350°F/180°C/Gas Mark 4 for about half an hour.

4 Leave to cool, slice into squares and serve.

Roshmalay

MOST SWEETS ORIGINATING IN INDIA ARE BASED ON DAIRY PRODUCTS, BUT HERE IS A DAIRY-FREE
VERSION OF AN EXOTIC TREAT.

2 cups/1 pound/455g medium or
firm tofu

2 cups/15 fl oz/425ml soy milk

2 tablespoons/1 oz/30g vegan
margarine

6 cardamom pods

½ cup/2 oz/55g slivered almonds

⅛ teaspoon freshly ground nutmeg

¾–1 cup/4–6 oz/115–170g raw
cane sugar

2 teaspoons rosewater

½ teaspoon vanilla extract

8 tablespoons water

1 Put the tofu into a clean dish towel and squeeze until as
much liquid as possible has been removed. Place the tofu in
a mixing bowl and knead briefly. Form into small balls about
the size of walnuts and set aside.

2 Bring the milk and margarine to a boil in a saucepan.
Remove the seeds from the cardamoms, grind them and add
to the saucepan with the almonds, nutmeg, and half the
sugar. Turn the heat down to fairly low and simmer,
uncovered, for 10–15 minutes. Remove from the heat, add
the rosewater and vanilla extract, and leave to cool.

3 In a small saucepan combine the water and the remaining
sugar, bring to a boil and cook, uncovered, over a medium
heat for about 15 minutes. Dip the tofu balls into this syrup
and place on a plate to cool.

4 Put the tofu balls into serving bowls, pour the milk mixture
over them and chill thoroughly until ready to serve.

Rich Desserts

Ideal to serve at dinner parties or celebrations, no one would guess that these sumptuous desserts are low-fat dairy-free alternatives. If you're looking for a rich dessert dish then this selection will not disappoint!

Raspberry Cheesecake

THIS RECIPE CONTAINS HONEY.

$^1/_3$ cup/1$^1/_2$ oz/45g rolled oats

$^1/_6$ cup/$^1/_2$ oz/15g shredded coconut

1 tablespoon vegan margarine

1$^1/_2$ cups/$^3/_4$ pound/340g firm tofu

2 tablespoons soy yogurt

2 tablespoons raw cane sugar

Juice and rind of $^1/_2$ orange

$^1/_2$ teaspoon vanilla extract

2 teaspoons tahini

Pinch of sea salt

2–3 tablespoons honey

4 tablespoons water

$^1/_8$ teaspoon powdered agar-agar

4 oz/115g fresh or defrosted frozen
    raspberries

1 Mix the oats and coconut together. Spread the margarine over the bottom of a pie pan, then sprinkle the oat and coconut mixture over it. Set aside.

2 Combine the tofu, yogurt, sugar, orange juice and rind, vanilla extract, tahini, and salt in a liquidizer. Blend thoroughly. Pour into the pie pan.

3 Melt the honey in the water in a small pan over a medium heat and dissolve the agar-agar in it. Bring to a boil then simmer for about 1 minute. Remove from the heat and stir in the raspberries. Pour over the tofu mixture in the pie pan.

4 Bake in the oven at 350°F/180°C, Gas Mark 4 for 35 minutes. Chill for several hours before serving.

Classic Cheesecake

BASE

1 cup/4 oz/115g whole-wheat flour

2 tablespoons/1 oz/30g raw cane sugar

Pinch of sea salt

Pinch of ground cinnamon

1/4 cup/2 oz/55g vegan margarine

1 tablespoon water

FILLING

1 1/4 cups/10 oz/285g firm tofu

2 tablespoons vegetable oil

4 tablespoons/2 oz/55g raw cane sugar

Juice and rind of 1 lemon

1 teaspoon vanilla extract

1/3 cup/1 1/2 oz/45g ground almonds

1/3 cup/2 oz/55g raisins or golden
    seedless raisins

1 To make the base, mix the flour, sugar, salt, and cinnamon together in a bowl. Rub the margarine in finely. Finally, work in the water. Transfer the mixture to an oiled pie pan and pat down lightly. Bake in the oven for 10 minutes at 350°F/180°C/Gas Mark 4.

2 Meanwhile, put the tofu, oil, sugar, lemon juice and rind, and vanilla extract into a liquidizer or food processor and blend thoroughly. Stir in the ground almonds and raisins.

3 Remove the base from the oven and spoon the filling evenly over the top. Return to the oven and bake for 30 minutes. Cool, then chill before serving.

Chocolate-topped Pie

1 cup/4 oz/115g whole-wheat flour
Pinch of sea salt
$^1/_4$ cup/2 oz/55g vegan margarine
$1^1/_2$ cups/$^3/_4$ pound/340g medium tofu
$^1/_2$ cup/3 oz/85g raw cane sugar
$1^1/_2$ teaspoons vanilla extract
1 tablespoon vegetable oil
$1^1/_2$ oz/45g semi-sweet chocolate
1 tablespoon cornstarch
4 tablespoons water

1 Put the flour and salt in a bowl, blend in the margarine, and add enough water to make a dough. Roll it out, put it into a pie pan, prick with a fork, and bake in the oven at 425°F/220°C/Gas Mark 7 for 10 minutes. Remove from the oven.

2 Put the tofu, all the sugar except 1 tablespoon, 1 teaspoon of the vanilla extract, and the oil in a liquidizer and blend thoroughly. Pour into the partially-baked pie shell, return to the oven and bake at 350°F/180°C/Gas Mark 4 for half an hour.

3 Melt the chocolate in a bowl over a saucepan of boiling water. Stir in the remaining sugar and vanilla extract. Dissolve the cornstarch in the water and stir into the chocolate. Continue stirring until the mixture has thickened.

4 Spoon the chocolate mixture over the baked pie. Leave to cool, then chill until ready to serve.

Maple Walnut Ice Cream

VEGAN ICE CREAMS ARE NOW AVAILABLE AT MANY HEALTH FOOD SHOPS, BUT FOR GREATER SCOPE AN ICE CREAM MAKER IS A BIG ADVANTAGE. IF YOU WANT TO TRY ONE OF THESE RECIPES WITHOUT ONE, THEN WHILE THE MIXTURE IS FREEZING, TAKE IT OUT EVERY 15–20 MINUTES AND STIR IT WELL.

¼ cup/2 oz/55g soft or medium tofu
⅔ cup/5 fl oz/140ml soy milk
2 tablespoons/1 oz/30g soft vegetarian
   margarine
⅔ cup/5 fl oz/140ml maple essence
1 teaspoon vanilla syrup
Pinch of sea salt
½ cup/2 oz/55g walnut pieces

1 Put all the ingredients except the walnut pieces into a liquidizer and blend thoroughly.
2 Stir in the walnut pieces (if they are large then break or chop them into small pieces).
3 Freeze in an ice cream maker. Otherwise, pour the mixture into a suitable container and put in a freezer. Stir frequently while it is freezing to avoid crystallization.

Coconut Milk Ice Cream

1 can (14 fl oz/400ml) coconut milk
2 tablespoons/1 oz/30g whole-wheat
   flour
⅙–⅓ cup/1–2 oz/30–55g raw
   cane sugar
1 teaspoon vanilla extract

1 Empty the contents of the can into a liquidizer, add the flour and sugar, and blend thoroughly. Transfer to a saucepan and heat gently until slightly thickened and simmering. Remove from the heat, cool, and chill thoroughly.
2 Stir the vanilla extract into the mixture, then pour into ice cream maker as per manufacturer's instructions.

Mint Choc Chip Ice Cream

THIS IS NOT BY ANY STRETCH OF THE IMAGINATION A "WHOLEFOOD" RECIPE, BUT ONCE IN A WHILE IT IS NICE TO INDULGE IN SOMETHING LIKE THIS. CHILDREN (OF ALL AGES) WILL LOVE IT. IF YOU CHECK THE INGREDIENTS OF MOST PEPPERMINT STICKS YOU WILL FIND THEY ARE VEGAN.

2 oz/55g peppermint stick
²/₃ cup/5 fl oz/140ml soy milk
²/₃ cup/5 fl oz/140ml Mock Cream
   (see page 244)
¹/₂ oz/15g vegan chocolate

1 Crush the peppermint stick. Soak the crushed peppermint stick in the soy milk for several hours.

2 Add the Mock Cream to the soy milk mixture and stir well. Chop the chocolate into very small pieces and add it to the mixture.

3 Proceed according to the instructions on your ice cream maker.

Hungarian Layered Pancakes

THIS IS UNDOUBTEDLY A TIME-CONSUMING RECIPE, BUT FOR ANYONE WITH A STRONGLY DEVELOPED SWEET TOOTH THE RESULTS CANNOT FAIL TO IMPRESS.

BATTER

1¼ cups/5 oz/140g whole-wheat flour

2 tablespoons soy flour

1 teaspoon baking powder

Pinch of sea salt

2 teaspoons vegetable oil plus
  additional for frying

½ cup/4 oz/115g firm or medium tofu

2 teaspoons raw cane sugar

1 tablespoon soy yogurt

2 teaspoons lemon juice

Grated rind of ½ lemon

3–4 tablespoons apricot preserves

½ cup/2 oz/55g hazelnuts, almonds,
  or walnuts

2 oz/55g semi-sweet chocolate

2 tablespoons/1 oz/30g creamed
  coconut

1 tablespoon hot water

Bottled chocolate sauce (optional)

1 To make the batter, mix the flour, soy flour, baking powder, and salt together in a bowl. Add the 2 teaspoons oil, then add a little water at a time, mixing in with a fork until the mixture is the consistency of thick cream. Leave it to stand for half an hour or more. (If it is then too thick add a little more water; if too thin a little more flour.)

2 Mash the tofu in a bowl. Stir in the sugar, yogurt, lemon juice, and lemon rind.

3 Heat the preserves slightly.

4 Grind the nuts finely. Grate the chocolate. Mix the ground nuts and chocolate together.

5 Fry the pancakes on both sides in a little oil. Place the first pancake on an oiled pie dish. Spread a layer of the tofu mixture on top. Fry the next pancake; put it on top of the tofu mixture then spread with a layer of apricot preserves. Fry a third pancake, put it on top, and spread some of the nut and chocolate mixture on top. Continue layering until all the ingredients have been used, finishing up with a pancake on top.

6 Grate or finely chop the creamed coconut and mix with the hot water. Spread over the top pancake. Bake in the oven at 375°F/190°C/Gas Mark 5 for 15–20 minutes.

7 Remove from the oven and slice into 4 wedges. Serve hot, with a bottled chocolate sauce poured over the top if desired.

Sweet Tofu Fritters

AN EXOTIC DESSERT WHICH IS NOT DIFFICULT TO MAKE. ORANGE FLOWER WATER IS AVAILABLE AT SPECIALIST DELICATESSENS AND FOOD HALLS.

1 cup/½ pound/225g firm tofu
½ cup/2 oz/55g whole-wheat flour
1 tablespoon honey
2 teaspoons orange flower water
Vegetable oil for deep-frying as required
½ pound/225g apricot preserves
4 tablespoons water

1. Mash the tofu in a mixing bowl. Stir in the flour, honey, and 1 teaspoon of the orange flower water.
2. Form the tofu mixture into walnut-sized fritters and deep-fry in the oil until golden brown. Drain and keep warm.
3. Heat the apricot preserves in a small saucepan. Add the water and the remaining orange flower water. Bring to a boil.
4. Serve the fritters warm with the hot apricot sauce poured over them.

Chocolate and Lemon Bananas

VEGAN CHOCOLATE IS NOW BECOMING WIDELY AVAILABLE — LOOK FOR IT AMONGST THE HIGH-QUALITY CONTINENTAL CHOCOLATES (THEY WILL ALWAYS LIST INGREDIENTS). A QUICK RECIPE.

1 medium lemon
¼ cup/2 oz/55g vegan margarine (preferably unsalted)
½ cup/2 oz/55g confectioner's sugar
3 oz/85g vegan chocolate
4 ripe bananas
⅙ cup/½ oz/15g shredded coconut

1. Grate the lemon and squeeze out the juice. Beat the margarine and sugar together in a bowl and add the lemon rind and juice. Place the bowl in the refrigerator for half an hour or more.
2. Put the chocolate in a small bowl over a pan of hot water. Place over a gentle heat until the chocolate has melted.
3. Peel and halve the bananas lengthways. Spoon the lemon mixture between banana halves to sandwich them together. Spoon the melted chocolate over them and sprinkle the coconut on top.

Bread and "Butter" Pudding

THIS VEGAN VERSION OF AN OLD-FASHIONED DESSERT IS GOOD WARMING, COMFORT FOOD.

Vegan margarine as required

5–6 slices whole-wheat bread

$^1/_2$ cup/3 oz/85g raisins or golden seedless raisins

$^1/_6$–$^1/_3$ cup/1–2 oz/30–55g raw cane sugar

4 tablespoons water

2 tablespoons soy flour

$^1/_2$ teaspoon baking powder

2$^1/_2$ cups/20 fl oz/570ml soy milk

Grated nutmeg as required

1 Spread margarine on the slices of bread and cut them into strips. Layer the strips in an ovenproof dish with the dried fruit and sugar.

2 Beat the soy flour and baking powder into the water with a fork.

3 Heat the milk in a saucepan but remove from the heat before it boils. Beat in the soy flour mixture. Pour this over the bread. Grate some nutmeg over this and leave to soak for 20–30 minutes.

4 Bake at 350°F/180°C/Gas Mark 4 for about half an hour. Alternatively, cover with wax paper and microwave for 12 minutes. Leave for 2 minutes before turning out.

Traditional Scottish Cloutie Dumpling

THIS TRADITIONAL RECIPE IS PERFECT FOR A COLD WINTER NIGHT. IT MAKES FOUR SERVINGS FOR THOSE WITH LARGE APPETITES; OTHERWISE IT COULD EASILY SERVE SIX.

¾ cup/3 oz/85g medium oatmeal

¾ cup/3 oz/85g whole-wheat flour

⅓ cup/3 oz/85g hard vegetable fat or shredded vegetable suet

½ cup/3 oz/85g raw cane sugar

⅘ cup/4 oz/115g golden seedless raisins, raisins, currants, or a mixture

1 teaspoon ground cinnamon

½ teaspoon baking soda

½–⅔ cup/4–5 oz/115–140g soy yogurt

Water as required

1 Put the oatmeal and flour in a mixing bowl. Grate the fat if not already shredded and add to the bowl. Add the sugar, dried fruit, cinnamon, and baking soda and mix well.

2 Add the yogurt and enough water to make a thick batter. Spoon the batter into an oiled pudding basin and steam for 2–3 hours. Alternatively, microwave for 12 minutes then leave to rest for 2 minutes before turning out. Serve with custard.

Steamed Preserves Pudding

1½ cups/6 oz/170g whole-wheat self-rising flour

½ cup/2 oz/55g soy flour

⅓ cup/2 oz/55g raw cane sugar

⅓–½ cup/3–4 oz/85–115g vegan margarine

Soy milk as required

Sugar-free or raw-sugar preserves as required

1 Mix the flour and sugar and rub in the margarine.
2 Add enough milk to make a soft dough.
3 Put some preserves at the bottom of a pudding basin and add the pudding mixture.
4 Cover with wax paper or aluminum foil and steam for 1 hour. Alternatively, cover with wax paper and microwave for 6–7 minutes.
5 Serve with custard if desired.

Baked Raisin Pudding

THIS IS ANOTHER WINTER PUDDING, BUT THIS TIME COOKED IN THE OVEN, THEREFORE REQUIRING LESS TIME.

⅔ cup/4 oz/115g raw cane sugar

2 tablespoons/1 oz/30g vegan margarine

½–⅔ cup/3–4 oz/85–115g raisins

¾ cup/7 fl oz/200ml boiling water

1 teaspoon vanilla extract

¾ cup/3 oz/85g whole-wheat flour

1 teaspoon baking powder

Approximately 5 tablespoons soy milk

3 tablespoons/1 oz/30g chopped nuts

1 First make a syrup by putting half the sugar, half the margarine, and the raisins in a small saucepan with the boiling water. Heat slowly until the sugar dissolves, then boil steadily for 10 minutes. Add the vanilla extract.
2 Meanwhile, beat the rest of the sugar and margarine together, add the flour mixed with the baking powder, and stir in enough milk to make a thick batter consistency.
3 Turn the mixture into an oiled ovenproof dish, pour the hot sauce over the top, and sprinkle with nuts.
4 Bake in a moderate oven at 350°F/180°C/Gas Mark 4 for 30 minutes. Serve immediately.

Coconut Cream Pie

CARTONS OF SOY-BASED DESSERTS ARE AVAILABLE UNDER AT LEAST TWO DIFFERENT BRANDS IN MANY HEALTH FOOD STORES. THEY ARE DELICIOUS ON THEIR OWN, BUT THE VANILLA ONE, IN PARTICULAR, MAY BE USED AS THE BASIS FOR OTHER DESSERTS. FOR AN AUTHENTIC FINISH TO THIS ONE, TOP IT WITH MOCK CREAM (SEE PAGE 244).

1 carton soy vanilla dessert
1 cup/3 oz/85g shredded coconut
1 pre-baked pie shell

1 Empty the contents of the carton into a saucepan and heat gently to boiling point. (Be careful not to burn it.) Simmer for a few minutes, then remove from the heat and stir in the coconut.

2 Leave the mixture to cool for a few minutes, then pour into a pie shell and refrigerate until ready to serve.

Oliebollen

THIS IS A TRADITIONAL DUTCH NEW YEAR'S EVE DISH WHICH ALTHOUGH SUGAR-FREE IS TRADITIONALLY SERVED WITH SUGAR OVER IT. THIS RECIPE SPECIFIES RAW CANE SUGAR BUT YOU COULD USE CONFECTIONER'S SUGAR IF YOU PREFER.

1½ cups/6 oz/170g whole-wheat flour

2 teaspoons dried yeast

1 apple

About 1⅓ cups/10 fl oz/285ml soy milk

⅓ cup/2 oz/55g raisins

⅓ cup/2 oz/55g currants

1 oz/30g candied mixed peel

3 teaspoons lemon juice

Pinch of sea salt

Vegetable oil for deep frying as required

Raw cane sugar as required

1 Put the flour in a bowl. If using "easybake" yeast it can be added straight to the bowl; otherwise dissolve it in a little of the milk.

2 Peel and chop the apple. Heat the milk to lukewarm.

3 Add the dried fruit, lemon juice, lemon, salt, and milk to the bowl. (The dough should be thick, so add the milk slowly and if it looks like becoming thin do not use the full amount.)

4 Cover the bowl and leave it in a warm place for an hour.

5 Drop spoonfuls of the dough in hot oil until lightly browned. Serve warm, sprinkled with sugar.

Sugar-Free Desserts

As well as being low in fat, the recipes that follow are totally free from added sugar so as desserts come, these are some of the lowest calorie options you'll ever find. The source of sweetness in these dishes is all natural, and comes from fresh fruit and alternatives such as maple syrup.

Maple Pecan Tofu Cheesecake

TO AVOID RAW CANE SUGAR, USE A GRANOLA THAT HAS NONE ADDED FOR THE BASE OF THIS CHEESECAKE.

1 cup/4 oz/115g crunchy granola
2 tablespoons/1 oz/30g vegan
    margarine
1½ cups/¾ pound/340g tofu
2 tablespoons/1 oz/30g vegetable oil
¾ cup/½ pound/225g maple syrup
½ cup/2 oz/55g pecans

1 Grind the granola in a liquidizer. Melt the margarine and mix with the granola. Transfer to a pie dish and press down well.
2 Blend the tofu, oil, and maple syrup in a liquidizer. Chop the nuts and stir them in.
3 Pour the tofu mixture over the granola crust and bake at 350°F/180°C/Gas Mark 4 for 30–40 minutes until well risen and turning golden brown. Cool and then chill before serving.

Fresh Fruit Frozen Smoothie

THIS FROZEN FRUIT DESSERT IS QUICK AND EASY TO MAKE AND DOESN'T REQUIRE THE USE OF AN ICE CREAM MAKER.

4 peaches or ½ pineapple
2 large bananas
¾ cup/7 fl oz/200ml pineapple or
    orange juice
1 cup/6 oz/170g raisins
¾ cup/4 oz/115g pecans

1 Chop the peaches or pineapple and bananas and place the pieces in the freezer compartment of the refrigerator until frozen.
2 Pour the juice into the liquidizer, add the raisins and pecans and blend thoroughly.
3 Add the frozen fruit, a little at a time, blending thoroughly after each addition. Serve immediately.

Sugar-free Carob Smoothie

THIS IS FAST, SIMPLE, AND HIGHLY NUTRITIOUS. A QUICK RECIPE.

1¹/₃ cups/10 fl oz/285ml water
¹/₄ cup/1 oz/30g soy flour
³/₅ cup/3 oz/85g sunflower seeds
4 tablespoons carob powder
¹/₂ cup/3 oz/85g pitted dates
2 teaspoons vanilla extract

1 Place all the ingredients in the liquidizer and blend thoroughly.

Banana Cream Pie

TO MAKE THE PASTRY FOR THIS DESSERT SEE PAGE 65.

1 pre-baked pie shell
1 cup/6 oz/170g pitted dates
³/₄ cup/4 oz/115g cashews
4 teaspoons arrowroot
Pinch of sea salt
1 teaspoon vanilla extract
1¹/₃ cups/10 fl oz/285ml water
2 ripe bananas

1 Chop the dates and place them in a liquidizer with the cashews, arrowroot, salt, vanilla extract, and water. Blend thoroughly.
2 Pour into the saucepan and heat gently, stirring constantly, until thickened. Allow the mixture to cool.
3 Slice the bananas into the pie shell. Cover them with the cashew-date mixture; chill and serve.

Avocado, Coconut, and Apple Dessert

2 sweet apples
Juice of ½ lemon
Juice of ½ orange
¼ cup/2 oz/55g creamed coconut
⅓ cup/2 oz/55g pitted dates
3 tablespoons/1 oz/30g walnut pieces
1 avocado

1 Peel and chop the apples. Place in a liquidizer with lemon and orange juice.
2 Grate the coconut. Chop the dates. Add both to the liquidizer together with the walnuts.
3 Peel and chop the avocado. Add the liquidizer and blend thoroughly.

Baked Date and Coconut Layer Cake

THIS IS A RICH DESSERT SWEETENED ONLY BY THE DATES.

2 cups/12 oz/340g pitted dates
1 cup/3 oz/85g shredded coconut
½ cup/4 oz/115g creamed coconut
1 teaspoon agar-agar
1⅓ cups/10 fl oz/285ml boiling water

1 Chop the dates finely. Place alternate layers of chopped dates and shredded coconut in an oiled casserole dish.
2 Grate or finely chop the creamed coconut and put it in a liquidizer with the agar-agar. Pour in the boiling water and blend thoroughly.
3 Pour the liquid over the dates and coconut.
4 Bake in a slow oven at 300°F/150°C/Gas Mark 2 for about 30 minutes or until brown on top. Serve hot.

Date and Coconut Crème

THIS TOO IS SWEETENED ONLY BY DATES BUT IT IS A REFRESHING COLD DESSERT.

¹/₂ cup/4 oz/115g creamed coconut
1¹/₃ cups/10 fl oz/285ml hot water
1 cup/6 oz/170g pitted dates
1 teaspoon vanilla extract

1 Grate or chop the creamed coconut finely and add it to the hot water in a saucepan.
2 Chop the dates and add them to the saucepan.
3 Cook the mixture over the lowest possible heat, stirring occasionally, until the dates have dissolved and the mixture is thick and creamy. Add the vanilla extract.
4 Chill thoroughly before serving.

Strawberry Ice Cream

1 cup/¹/₂ pound/225g soft or
   medium tofu
4 tablespoons soy milk
2 oz/55g raw cane sugar
2 tablespoons vegetable oil
Pinch of sea salt
¹/₂ pound/225g fresh or defrosted
   frozen raspberries
1 teaspoon lemon juice
¹/₂ teaspoon vanilla extract
2–3 drops almond extract

1 Put the tofu, milk, sugar, oil, and salt in a liquidizer and blend thoroughly.
2 Sieve the raspberries, discard the seeds, and add this purée to the liquidizer along with the lemon juice, vanilla and almond extracts. Blend thoroughly.
3 Freeze in an ice cream maker, or in a freezer following the instructions for Maple Walnut Ice Cream (see page 257).

Carob and Date Ice Cream

AS BEFORE, THIS RECIPE HAS NO ADDED SUGAR, BUT THE CREAM IS ALREADY SWEETENED. NOT EVERYONE HAS AN ICE CREAM MAKER AND THIS DESSERT CAN EASILY BE MADE WITHOUT ONE.

1 cup/6 oz/170g pitted dates
2 cups/15 fl oz/425ml water
4 tablespoons vegetable oil
1/4 cup/1 oz/30g carob powder
2 teaspoons vanilla extract
2 cartons (4 oz/125g each) soy cream

1 Soak the dates in the water for several hours (not absolutely necessary, but it does make blending easier). Blend all the ingredients in a liquidizer and place the mixture in the freezer compartment of the refrigerator for at least 3 hours, stirring occasionally.

Maple Raisin Tart

THIS RECIPE ALLOWS YOU TO INDULGE IN SOMETHING AS YUMMY AS PURE MAPLE SYRUP AND YET FEEL VIRTUOUS BECAUSE YOU ARE NOT EATING SUGAR.

1/2 cup/4 fl oz/120ml water
1 1/2 tablespoons cornstarch
1 cup/12 oz/340g maple syrup
1 cup/6 oz/170g raisins
1 quantity Whole-wheat Pastry
   (see page 65)

1 Blend the water and cornstarch in a liquidizer and pour it into a saucepan. Stir in the maple syrup and raisins and bring to a boil, stirring constantly until it thickens, then continue cooking over a very low heat for two or three minutes more, until it becomes transparent.

2 Roll out most of the pastry and place it in a pan. Cool the mixture slightly and pour it into a pastry case. Cover with a lattice top made from remaining strips of pastry.

3 Bake for about 20 minutes in a hot oven 425°F/225°C/Gas Mark 7 until the pastry is lightly browned. Serve warm.

Maple Cobbler

2 cups/¹/₂ pound/225g whole-wheat
   flour
4 teaspoons baking powder
Pinch of sea salt
¹/₄ cup/2 oz/55g vegan margarine
About ²/₃ cup/5 fl oz/140ml soy milk
1¹/₃ cups/1 pound/455g maple syrup

1 Combine the flour, baking powder, and salt in a bowl. Mix in the margarine. Add the milk and stir just enough to moisten the dry ingredients. (Different flours require different amounts of liquid, so if it is too dry to knead into a dough then add a little more milk.)

2 Knead the dough gently, then roll it out to a thickness of about ¹/₂ inch/1.25cm and cut it into squares, rectangles or circles.

3 Heat the syrup to boiling point and pour it into a baking dish. Put the dough pieces on top of the syrup and bake uncovered in a hot oven 425°F/225°C/Gas Mark 7 for 15–20 minutes, until the surface is golden brown, basting once with the syrup before the end of the cooking time.

Date and Pecan Cake

THIS OLD-FASHIONED-STYLE WHOLE-WHEAT CAKE IS VERY QUICK AND EASY TO MAKE.

1$^1/_3$ cups/$^1/_2$ pound/225g pitted dates

$^1/_3$ cup/2 oz/55g pecans

$^1/_3$ cup/3 oz/85g vegan margarine

1$^1/_3$ cups/10 fl oz/285ml water

$^3/_4$ cup/4 oz/115g raisins

$^1/_2$ teaspoon ground cinnamon

$^1/_2$ teaspoon nutmeg

Pinch of sea salt

2 cups/$^1/_2$ pound/225g whole-wheat flour

1 teaspoon baking powder

1 teaspoon baking soda

1 Chop the dates and pecans.

2 Put the dates, margarine, water, and raisins in a large saucepan. Bring to a boil and then let it boil for a couple of minutes.

3 Remove from the cooker and stir in the remaining ingredients, mixing thoroughly. Turn the mixture into a cake pan and bake at 375°F/190°C/Gas Mark 5 for about 45 minutes.

Applesauce Cake

MAPLE SYRUP CAN BE USED AS A GLAZE, BRUSHED OVER THE CAKE ONCE COOLED.

6 oz/170g cooking apples

³/₄ cup/4 oz/115g pitted dates

3 tablespoons water

¹/₄ cup/2 oz/55g vegan margarine

1 teaspoon baking soda

1¹/₂ cups/6 oz/170g self-rising whole-wheat flour

1 teaspoon ground cinnamon

Grating nutmeg

1 Peel and chop the apples. Chop the dates. Put the chopped apple and dates into a saucepan with the water. Bring to a boil, then lower the heat, cover and cook until the apple is tender. Cool slightly then put the mixture into a liquidizer and blend thoroughly.

2 Return the apple mixture to the saucepan and heat again over a very low heat. Add the margarine and stir until it is melted. Remove from the heat and immediately stir in the soda.

3 Add the flour, cinnamon, and a good grating of nutmeg to the pan and stir quickly just until it is all mixed.

4 Transfer the batter to a cake pan and bake at 350°F/180°C/Gas Mark 4 for about 40 minutes.

Honeyed Tofu and Yogurt Pie

1–1¹/₂ cups/¹/₂–³/₄ pound/225–340g firm tofu

1¹/₃ cups/10 fl oz/285ml soy yogurt

4 tablespoons honey

1 teaspoon vanilla extract

1 pre-baked whole-wheat pastry shell

Fresh fruit (e.g. strawberries, bananas, peaches, kiwi fruit) as required

1 Put the tofu into a clean dish towel and squeeze until the liquid has been extracted. Put into a mixing bowl and add the yogurt, honey, and vanilla extract. Beat well.

2 Spoon the tofu mixture into the baked pie shell, cover and chill for several hours.

3 When ready to serve top with sliced fresh fruit.

Fresh Fruit Desserts

Fruit is a delight you can eat at any time – with the knowledge that you're giving your body a vitamin, mineral, and antioxidant boost it will thank you for. These fresh fruit-based dessert dishes provide exciting new ways to make use of a wide range of different fruits.

Apricot Cream

1 cup/4–6 oz/115–170g dried apricots

1–1¹⁄₂ cups/¹⁄₂–³⁄₄ pound/225–340g
   medium or firm tofu

2–3 teaspoon lemon juice

4 tablespoons/2 oz/55g raw cane sugar

2 tablespoons soy yogurt

3–4 tablespoons slivered almonds

1 Soak the apricots in water for several hours or steam until
   tender (apricots that have been cooked will give a creamier
   texture; apricots that have simply been soaked will have a
   chewier texture).

2 Combine all the ingredients, except the almonds, in a
   liquidizer and blend thoroughly.

3 Pour into dessert dishes and top with the almonds.
   Serve chilled.

Pineapple Crème

THIS RECIPE CONTAINS HONEY, THOUGH YOU COULD SUBSTITUTE SUGAR TO TASTE.

1 can (14 oz–16oz/400g) pineapple in
   its own juice

1¹⁄₂ cups/³⁄₄ pound/340g medium tofu

¹⁄₆ cup/2 oz/55g honey

1 tablespoon vegetable oil

1 Put the pineapple into a liquidizer with the tofu, honey, oil,
   and about 1 tablespoon juice from the can. Blend
   thoroughly.

2 Pour into dessert dishes and chill well before serving.

Baked Banana Rolls with Hot Lemon Sauce

FOR THE ROLLS

$^1/_2$ quantity Whole-wheat Pastry (see
  page 65)

4 small bananas

2 tablespoons raw cane sugar

Ground cinnamon as required

FOR THE SAUCE

$^1/_2$ cup/3 oz/85g raw cane sugar

$^3/_4$–1 cup/7–8 fl oz/200–225ml water

1 tablespoon cornstarch

Juice of 1 lemon

1 Make the pastry and roll out into 4 oblong shapes.
2 Peel the bananas and place one on each of the pastry strips. Sprinkle each with $^1/_2$ tablespoon sugar and a little cinnamon, then fold over the pastry to enclose the banana. Place on an oiled baking sheet and bake for 15 minutes at 400°F/200°C/Gas Mark 8.
3 Meanwhile, put the sugar and water in a saucepan and bring to a boil slowly. Mix the cornstarch with the lemon juice and stir it into the saucepan. Continue stirring constantly until the mixture has thickened. Simmer briefly so that any raw floury taste disappears. Alternatively, mix the lemon juice, sugar, and cornstarch together and stir in the water, microwave for 1 minute, then stir and microwave again until the sugar has melted and the sauce thickened.
4 Serve the pastry parcels with sauce poured over them.

Blueberry Sorbet

3 cups/1 pound/455g fresh blueberries

Juice of 2 lemons

$^1/_2$–$^2/_3$ cup/3–4 oz/85–115g raw cane
  sugar

1 Clean the blueberries.
2 Purée the fruit (in 2 batches if necessary) in a liquidizer.
3 Add the lemon juice to the sugar and stir well. Mix this in with the fruit purée.
4 Freeze the mixture in the ice compartment of the refrigerator. If desired, when almost stiff, purée again in a liquidizer just before serving.

Fresh Fruit Trifle

THIS IS A DESSERT WHICH MOST PEOPLE WHO BECOME VEGAN THINK THEY WILL NEVER BE ABLE TO EAT AGAIN.

225g/½ pound plain sponge cake (see page 245)

1 pound/455g fresh fruit

1 package vegan fruit jelly

Custard powder as required

Raw cane sugar as required

2½ cups/20 fl oz/570ml soy milk

1 Crumble the cake into the bottom of the dish.

2 Chop the fruit and put it on top of the cake.

3 Make up the jelly according to the directions on the package and pour it over the cake and fruit.

4 Make up a thick custard with the milk and when the jelly has set, spread this over the top.

5 Leave in the refrigerator for several hours before serving.

Nutty Apple Mousse

COOKED APPLES, LEMON, AND CASHEWS ARE A VERY APPEALING COMBINATION.

⅔ cup/3 oz/85g cashews

1 pound/455g cooking apples

⅔ cup/4 oz/115g raw cane sugar

1⅓ cups/10 fl oz/285ml water

1 teaspoon agar-agar

Juice of 1 lemon

1 Grind the cashews finely.

2 Peel and slice the apples and cook them with the sugar in just enough of the water to cover. When tender, add the rest of the water and bring to a boil.

3 Sprinkle the agar-agar carefully into the saucepan and cook for 1 minute.

4 Pour the mixture into a liquidizer. Add the lemon juice and ground cashews and blend them thoroughly.

5 Pour into a serving dish or four individual dishes and leave the mousse to cool, then chill before serving.

Baked Nutty Apples

THIS IS A GOOD DESSERT TO MAKE WHEN USING THE OVEN FOR A SAVORY DISH (IT IS MUCH QUICKER THAN CONVENTIONAL BAKED APPLES AND NEEDS A MUCH LOWER OVEN HEAT). SERVE WITH A VEGAN CREAM OR CUSTARD.

¼ cup/2 oz/55g vegan margarine
½ cup/3 oz/85g raw cane sugar
½ cup/2 oz/55g whole-wheat flour
3 tablespoons/1 oz/30g slivered almonds or chopped walnuts
4 cooking apples

1 Beat the margarine with the sugar, then mix in the flour and nuts.
2 Peel and core the apples and halve them. Arrange them, flat side up, in an oiled baking dish. Spoon some of the sugar mixture on top of each.
3 Bake the apples uncovered in a moderate oven, 350°F/180°C/Gas Mark 4 for about half an hour until the apples are soft.

Summer Fruit Cup

A VEGAN WITH A SWEET TOOTH CAN GET PRETTY FED UP WITH BEING OFFERED NOTHING BUT FRUIT SALADS FOR DESSERT, BUT THIS ONE IS IN A CLASS OF ITS OWN. SUITABLE FOR A DINNER PARTY.

¾ cup/7 fl oz/200ml orange juice
¾ cup/7 fl oz/200ml water
⅓ cup/2 oz/55g raw cane sugar
½ teaspoon ground cinnamon
2 small oranges
2 ripe peaches
6–8 oz/170–225g strawberries
3 tablespoons/1 oz/30g chopped almonds

1 Cook the orange juice, water, sugar, and cinnamon until it begins to thicken into a syrup. Set aside to cool.
2 Peel and segment the orange; slice the peaches and strawberries.
3 Combine the fruit in a bowl and pour the syrup over them. Sprinkle with the almonds. Chill before serving.

Hot Blackberry Soup

ON THE CONTINENT FRUIT SOUP IS OFTEN EATEN AS AN APPETIZER IN SUMMER, BUT IT ALSO MAKES A GOOD DESSERT. THIS RECIPE ALSO WORKS WITH RASPBERRIES AND IS USUALLY EATEN WITH COOKIES.

5 cups/40 fl oz/1120ml water
1½ pound/680g fresh blackberries
¼ cup/2 oz/55g vegan margarine
1½ tablespoons whole-wheat flour
⅓ cup/2 oz/55g raw cane sugar
3 tablespoons/1 oz/30g chopped almonds

1 Put the water in a saucepan and add the berries. Bring to a boil and simmer until tender, then put them through a sieve. Return the sieved berries to the cooking liquid; discard the pulp.
2 Heat the margarine in a pan and stir in the flour. Add the soup gradually, stirring constantly to avoid lumps. Sweeten (the amount given is only a rough guide as berries vary so much in sweetness) and simmer for about 10 minutes.
3 Serve hot, sprinkled with almonds.

Quick Cook Bananas and Oranges

IF YOU ARE USING THE OVEN FOR A SAVORY DISH, WHEN YOU REMOVE IT JUST POP THIS IN FOR A SIMPLE DESSERT. A QUICK RECIPE.

2 tablespoons/1 oz/30g vegan margarine
¼ cup/1½ oz/45g raw cane sugar
2 oranges
4 bananas

1 Grate the zest of one of the oranges. Beat the margarine and sugar together and mix in the grated rind.
2 Peel and slice the oranges. Peel and slice the bananas. Layer the fruit and the margarine mixture in a baking dish, and bake at 425°F/220°C/Gas Mark 7 for 10 minutes.

Austrian Apple Strudel

WITH FROZEN FILO PASTRY SO EASILY AVAILABLE THIS DESSERT HAS BECOME SOMETHING YOU CAN PREPARE YOURSELF IN NO TIME AT ALL. THIS IS NICE WITH A LITTLE CONFECTIONER'S SUGAR SPRINKLED OVER THE TOP AND/OR SOME VEGAN CREAM.

1 pound/455g cooking apples

$\frac{1}{2}$ cup/3 oz/85g raw cane sugar

$\frac{1}{3}$ cup/1 oz/55g raisins or golden seedless raisins

$\frac{1}{4}$ cup/1 oz/30g slivered almonds

$\frac{1}{2}$ teaspoon ground cinnamon

$\frac{1}{4}$ cup/2 oz/55g vegan margarine

4 sheets filo pastry (thawed)

1 Peel the apples and chop them finely. Put them in a bowl with the sugar, raisins, almonds, and cinnamon; mix well.

2 Melt the margarine. Mix about half of it into the apple mixture.

3 Brush each of the filo pastry sheets with some of the remaining margarine, then put a quarter of the apple mixture on each and roll the dough up.

4 Place the strudel on a baking sheet and bake at 375°F/190°C/Gas Mark 5 for about half an hour. Serve warm if possible.

Sweet Breakfast Dishes

The perfect way to start the day has to be with a hot, sweet breakfast. The breakfast ideas that follow are a pleasure to eat and to serve.

Waffles

THIS IS A FAIRLY CONVENTIONAL WAFFLE RECIPE BUT OF COURSE WITHOUT THE UNNECESSARY EGGS. SERVE THE WAFFLES WITH MAPLE SYRUP.

2 cups/½ pound/225g whole-wheat flour

1½ teaspoons baking powder

Pinch of sea salt

2 cups/15 fl oz/425ml soy milk

4 tablespoons vegetable oil

Chopped pecans as required (optional)

1 Place the flour in a large mixing bowl and add the baking powder and salt.

2 Gently stir in the milk and oil (and pecans if using). Prepare on a waffle iron.

Oat and Cashew Waffles

THIS MORE UNUSUAL WAFFLE RECIPE, WHICH REQUIRES NO RAISING AGENT, IS ALSO BEST SERVED WITH MAPLE SYRUP.

2 cups/½ pound/225g rolled oats

½ cup/3 oz/85g cashews

Pinch of sea salt

1 tablespoon vegetable oil

1 cup/8 fl oz/225ml water

1 Put the oats and cashews in a liquidizer and grind. Add the salt, oil, and water and blend thoroughly.

2 Pour the batter in a waffle iron and leave for a few minutes until cooked.

Hot Cakes

THESE ARE SIMILAR TO "SCOTCH" PANCAKES BUT RATHER THAN BEING BUTTERED THEY ARE SERVED PIPING HOT WITH MAPLE SYRUP.

2 cups/½ pound/225g whole-wheat flour
1 teaspoon baking powder
1 teaspoon baking soda
Pinch of sea salt
¾ cup/6 oz/170g soy yogurt
1 cup/8 fl oz/225ml water
2 tablespoons vegetable oil

1 Mix the flour, baking powder, baking soda, and salt in a bowl. Add the yogurt, water, and oil and stir briefly.
2 Fry the hot cakes in a heated skillet or griddle, flipping them over when done on one side.

Muffins

NOWADAYS MUFFINS ARE ALMOST AS SWEET AS CAKE, BUT IN THEIR ORIGINAL FORM THEY WERE ONLY SLIGHTLY SWEETENED AND SERVED WITH PRESERVES. THIS RECIPE MAKES ABOUT 2 DOZEN SMALL MUFFINS OR A DOZEN LARGE ONES.

2 cups/½ pound/225g whole-wheat flour
1 teaspoon baking powder
1 teaspoon baking soda
Pinch of sea salt
1–2 tablespoons raw cane sugar
3 tablespoons vegan margarine
2 cups/15 fl oz/425ml soy yogurt

1 Put all the dry ingredients in a bowl and mix them well.
2 Melt the margarine. Add it to the dry ingredients along with the yogurt. Stir the mixture until it is a smooth batter.
3 Pour the batter into an oiled muffin tray and bake at 425°F/225°C/Gas Mark 7 for 15–20 minutes.

No-Egg Crêpes

FILLED WITH PRESERVES, THESE CRÊPES ARE PERFECT FOR BREAKFAST. THEY CAN ALSO BE USED FOR SAVORY PANCAKES.

1½ cups/6 oz/170g whole-wheat flour

3 tablespoons soy flour

1 teaspoon baking powder

2 teaspoons vegetable oil

1 teaspoon sea salt

Water as required

1 Combine the flours, baking powder, and sea salt. Make a well in the center, pour in the oil, then pour in the water gradually, stirring constantly with a fork. The consistency should be like thick cream. Leave to stand for about half an hour. If it is too thick then add more water; if it is too thin, add more flour.

2 Melt some vegan margarine or vegetable oil in a skillet and fry the crêpes on both sides.

Blintzes

THIS IS A VEGAN VERSION OF A TRADITIONAL JEWISH DISH (MAKES 15–20 BLINTZES). SERVE THEM TOPPED WITH ADDITIONAL SUGAR AND YOGURT OR VEGAN SOUR CREAM.

Crêpe batter (see above)

2 cups/1 pound/455g tofu

2 tablespoons soy yogurt plus additional as required *or* 1 cup/½ pound/225g tofu and 1 cup/½ pound/225g vegan cream cheese

2 tablespoons raw cane sugar plus additional as required

1 teaspoon vanilla extract

Vegan margarine as required

1 Put the tofu into a clean dish towel and squeeze to extract the water. Transfer the dry tofu to a mixing bowl. Stir in the yogurt (or cream cheese, if using), sugar, and vanilla extract.

2 Fry each pancake in margarine on one side only. Fill with the tofu mixture on the cooked side and roll up.

3 When all the pancakes are filled, heat a little margarine in the skillet and fry the blintzes, turning them so that they are lightly browned on both sides.

French Toast

"FRENCH TOAST" IS ACTUALLY AMERICAN, AND IS TRADITIONALLY MADE WITH AN EGGY BATTER. TOFU GIVES THE SAME EFFECT. SERVE WITH MAPLE SYRUP, OR PRESERVES, OR A MIXTURE OF RAW CANE SUGAR AND GROUND CINNAMON.

1½ cups/12 oz/340g soft or medium tofu
1 cup/8 fl oz/225ml water
4 tablespoons vegetable oil
Pinch of sea salt
1 teaspoon vanilla extract
3–4 teaspoons raw cane sugar
8 slices whole-wheat bread
Margarine for frying as required

1 Put the tofu, water, oil, salt, vanilla extract, and sugar in a liquidizer and blend thoroughly. Pour the mixture into a shallow bowl and dip the slices of bread in it.
2 Heat a little margarine in a skillet and fry the bread over a moderate heat until browned on both sides.

Nutty French Toast

THIS IS A VARIANT ON THE TRADITIONAL FRENCH TOAST. SERVE WITH THE SAME TOPPINGS.

⅓ cup/2 oz/55g cashews
⅓ cup/2 oz/55g almonds
1⅓ cups/10 fl oz/285ml soy milk
8 slices whole-wheat bread
Vegan margarine or vegetable oil as required

1 Grind the cashews and almonds in a liquidizer. Add the milk and blend thoroughly.
2 Pour the nut and milk mixture into a shallow bowl and dip the bread slices in it.
3 Heat the margarine or oil and fry the coated bread, turning once so that it is golden brown on both sides. Serve immediately.